W9-CGV-206

Is There a Woman
in the House...or Senate?

Bryna J. Fireside

NATIONAL AMERICAN
WOMAN SUFFRAGE ASS'N

Jeannette Rankin speaks to suffragists, about 1917.

Albert Whitman & Company, Morton Grove, Illinois

For my daughter, Leela

Front cover: Jeannette Rankin, about 1903. The Schlesinger Library,
Radcliffe College.
Back cover: Rep. Patricia Schroeder visits a military base in 1987.
Courtesy of Rep. Patricia Schroeder.
p. 6: Courtesy of Shirley Chisholm, Geraldine Ferraro, Sen. Nancy
Kassebaum, Sen. Barbara Mikulski, and Rep. Patricia Schroeder.

Library of Congress Cataloging-in-Publication Data

Fireside, Bryna J.
   Is there a woman in the House...or Senate? / Bryna J. Fireside.
     p.   cm.
   Summary: Biographies of ten pathbreaking women who have served in
Congress: Jeannette Rankin, Margaret Chase Smith, Shirley Chisholm,
Bella Abzug, Barbara Jordan, Patricia Schroeder, Millicent Fenwick,
Barbara Mikulski, Nancy Kassebaum, and Geraldine Ferraro.
   ISBN 0–8075–3662–8
   1. Women legislators—United States—Biography—Juvenile
literature. 2. Legislators—United States—Biography—Juvenile
literature. 3. United States. Congress—Biography—Juvenile
literature. 4. United States—Politics and government—20th
century—Juvenile literature. [1. Women legislators.
2. Legislators. 3. United States. Congress—Biography.]
I. Title.
E747.F48 1994
328.73'0082—dc20   92–28286
[B]   CIP
                                             AC

The text of this book is set in Palatino.
Design by Karen A. Yops.
Text copyright © 1994 by Bryna J. Fireside.
Published in 1994 by Albert Whitman & Company,
6340 Oakton Street, Morton Grove, Illinois 60053–2723.
Published simultaneously in Canada
by General Publishing, Limited, Toronto.
Printed in the United States of America.
10 9 8 7 6 5 4 3 2 1

ACKNOWLEDGMENTS

It was my good fortune to be able to interview nine of the ten women who appear in this book. A thousand thanks to Bella Abzug, Shirley Chisholm, the late Millicent Fenwick, Geraldine Ferraro, Barbara Jordan, Nancy Kassebaum, Barbara Mikulski, Patricia Schroeder, and Margaret Chase Smith for taking time from their busy schedules to answer my questions. I thank former Congressman Matthew F. McHugh, who was my representative from the Twenty-eighth Congressional District in New York for eighteen years, and his able staff, both in Ithaca, New York, and Washington, D.C. They opened doors which might otherwise have been closed and sent me invaluable material.

Thank you, Sarah Parham, coordinator of special collections at Texas Southern University (TSU), Houston, Texas, for smoothing the way for an interview with Barbara Jordan. Thanks also to Professor Thomas Freeman, who was Barbara Jordan's debate coach at TSU; Professor Otis King, former dean of TSU's Thurgood Marshall Law School, who was Barbara Jordan's debating partner during her college years; and Dean Max Sherman of the Lyndon Baines Johnson School of Public Affairs, University of Texas at Austin, who served with Barbara Jordan in the Texas State Senate.

Many thanks as well to Gregory P. Gallant, director of the Northwood Institute, Skowhegan, Maine; Andrea Camp, press secretary to Congresswoman Pat Schroeder; Mike Morrell and John Steele, press secretaries to Senator Barbara Mikulski; Mike Horak, press secretary to Senator Nancy Kassebaum; and Larry Shaiman, former press secretary to Senator Kassebaum.

Additionally, I thank those wonderful reference librarians at Tompkins County Public Library in Ithaca, New York, who searched for obscure facts or difficult-to-find books for me. I am also grateful to the staffs of the National Archives, the Bureau of Engraving and Printing, and the library of *USA Today*, all in Washington, D.C.; and the staffs of the Olin Library at Cornell University, Ithaca, New York; the Schlesinger Library at Radcliffe College, Cambridge, Massachusetts; the Montana Historical Society in Helena, Montana; the Lyndon Baines Johnson Library of the National Archives, Austin, Texas; and the Robert J. Terry Library at TSU, Houston, Texas.

On the home front, I owe an extraspecial thank you to my friend and writing buddy, Metta Winter, who read and critiqued all my early drafts, and to my husband, Harvey Fireside, who traveled from Maine to Texas with me while I interviewed and did research, and helped with the index to this book. Thanks, too, to Professor Martin Brownstein of the politics department at Ithaca College, Ithaca, New York, for his help with the introduction. And, finally, thanks to my editor at Albert Whitman & Company, Abby Levine, who was generous with her praise, careful with her editing, and enormously supportive.

Pat Schroeder visits a military base in 1987.

TABLE OF CONTENTS

Mikulski
U.S. SENATE

PAID FOR BY MIKULSKI FOR SENATE

Pat Schroeder
She wins.
We win.
Congresswoman

Nancy 84 Senate

GERALDINE FERRARO
19 84
AMERICA'S FIRST WOMAN VICE PRES.

i IS
for CHIS
SHIRLEY CHISHOLM FOR PRESIDENT '72

Take the
CHISHOLM trail
to
1600
Pennsylvania Ave.

Catalyst
for change
CHISHOLM
for PRESIDENT
★ '72 ★

PAT SCHROEDER
19 88
PRESIDENT

Pat Schroeder
SHE WINS... WE WIN... AGAIN!

Paid for by Schroeder for Congress Committee Inc.

HOW CONGRESS WORKS

Have you ever heard your parents talk about the national elections? Or seen a television ad asking you to vote for Ms. Candidate for the House of Representatives or Mr. Electable for the United States Senate? Have you read a newspaper headline that says, "Congress Votes Aid to Hurricane Victims" or "President Asks Congress for More Money for Head Start Program"?

What's it all about? Why is being a member of Congress such an important thing? What does Congress do, anyway?

The most important job of Congress is to write the laws by which we live. The president has the right to veto (say no to) a law Congress passes, and Congress can refuse to pass a law the president wants.

Congress also decides how much money can be spent to carry out those laws. To pay for all the things our government does, Congress passes laws which say how much taxes people and businesses must pay.

How does Congress get to make all these important decisions? To find some of the answers, we look to our Constitution. The Constitution calls for our government to be divided into three parts: the *executive* branch (the president and his advisers), the *legislative* branch (the Congress), and the *judicial* branch (the Supreme Court and other federal courts). This *separation of powers* is important. It means that no one part becomes too powerful. And each branch of the government keeps an eye on the others. This is called a system of *checks and balances.*

The Constitution spells out exactly what the president's powers are. It says what the members of the Supreme Court may do. But the Constitution has the most to say about the job of Congress.

The Senate and the House of Representatives

According to the Constitution, Congress has two *chambers,* or parts: the House of Representatives and the Senate.

There are four hundred thirty-five members of the House of Representatives. How many representatives your state has depends on how many people live in it. This number is found by a national *census* (count of people) that the federal government takes every ten years. (A state may gain or lose representatives if population shifts.) Each state is divided into *congressional districts* of approximately five hundred seventy-five thousand people. Each congressional district can send one representative to Congress. You can only vote for the candidate running from your district.

House members are elected for two-year terms. Elections are held on the first Tuesday in November in even-numbered years (1994, 1996, 1998, 2000, etc.).

Each state sends two senators to Congress. There are fifty states, so the Senate has exactly one hundred members. They are elected by all the voters in their states to serve for six years. Although a senatorial term is six years, elections are held every two years, at the same time as the elections for the House. So at each election, about one-third of the members of the Senate are chosen.

All members of Congress report to work on January 3 of the year following the election. Old terms of office end at noon on January 3, and the new terms begin immediately afterward. (The January 3 date was established in 1933, by the Twentieth Amendment to the Constitution.) There is no limit to the number of terms a member of Congress may serve.

Besides writing laws, each chamber has other duties spelled out in the Constitution. Some duties are reserved just for the House of Representatives, and others just for the Senate.

Only members of the House of Representatives write the laws that have to do with taxing and spending. The Senate may then change or approve these laws. Only the House of Representatives decides if there is enough evidence of wrongdoing by a president, vice-president, member of the Supreme Court, or other government official to impeach (accuse) that person.

Only senators can vote to approve or disapprove any treaty the president makes with a foreign country. Only senators approve the people the president wants to appoint to the Supreme Court or other federal courts, or who serve in the president's cabinet. If enough senators vote no, the president has to choose someone else. Only senators can conduct a trial if the president, vice-president, member of the Supreme Court, or other government official has been impeached.

Congress has eighteen other powers according to the Constitution. These include the power to declare war, coin money, regulate trade with other countries, propose amendments (changes) to the Constitution, establish federal courts, protect the discoveries of inventors by issuing patents (special rights) to their inventions, admit new states to the Union, . . . and punish pirates!

Congress has important tasks that are not mentioned in the Constitution. Members of Congress meet with citizens in their Washington offices and in offices in their own districts back home. Many members of Congress hold town meetings in their districts to get voters' opinions and tell them what's going on in Washington. Congressional staffs, in Washington or back home, help people with their problems. And they listen to citizens' views and pass them along to the representative or senator. Members of Congress read reports researched by staff members and meet with them to discuss issues. They speak to schoolchildren and other groups. They attend official ceremonies and receptions and meet distinguished visitors from other countries. Sometimes, if there is a problem in a foreign country, a small group of members of Congress goes on a fact-finding mission and reports back to the rest of Congress and to the president.

Getting the Work Done

Almost all members of Congress belong to either the Democratic or Republican party, although smaller political parties occasionally elect their candidates.

Very often Democrats and Republicans don't agree on the best way to solve problems. Each party has a *platform*, or plan, which it presents to the people every four years, when there is a presidential election. For example, in 1992, presidential candidate Bill Clinton's plan was to make sure every American could get health care. Generally, Democrats want to pass laws in which the government will help pay for programs to provide for the "general welfare." And, generally, Republicans want people to get together to solve their own problems whenever possible. They believe, for example, that jobs are best provided through private businesses rather than by the federal government.

Often members of Congress vote the way the leaders of their party suggest. But they must also listen to the people who elected them. And finally, they must follow their consciences as to whether a particular law would be good or bad for the country.

There are differences in how members of Congress from different regions of the country think about problems. A representative from New York City may want to save the national forests in Oregon, while a senator from Oregon will worry about jobs lost if the loggers can't cut down trees. Or members of Congress may disagree on how much money the military needs, although they all agree that we need a strong military to protect our country.

With so many different opinions and interests, how can Congress, with its five hundred thirty-five members, get anything done?

Congressional leaders from each party are elected by their colleagues to help members work together and compromise on hard issues. In the House of Representatives, the party with the most members elects the *Speaker of the House.* The other party elects a *House Minority Leader.* The Senate also elects leaders from each party—the *Majority Leader* and *Minority Leader*. It is the job of the party leaders to get their members to agree on difficult issues among themselves and, later, with members of the other party.

Because there is so much to do in Congress, it would be impossible for each member to study every new law that is proposed. So the work of

Congress is organized by *committees* (small groups) and *subcommittees* (even smaller groups within the committee). There are twenty-two permanent committees in the House of Representatives and sixteen in the Senate. Other committees are organized when necessary. Members generally serve on two or at most three committees at one time. This way they become experts in certain areas, such as education, science, or foreign affairs. Then when it comes time to vote on a particular bill, their colleagues will respect the recommendations of their party members on the committee.

How a Bill Becomes Law

The main job of Congress is to make laws. There are special rules for how this happens.

All *bills* (which is what they are called at first) start with an idea. Let's follow a bill through the House of Representatives. First, a representative submits his or her idea to the *House Legislative Council*. The council makes sure that the idea is legal and that no similar bill has been passed. The idea is typed up on the proper piece of paper in the right kind of language. Then the *sponsor* (creator) of the bill sends a letter around to his or her colleagues to see if others will co-sponsor the bill. Next, the bill's sponsor goes onto the floor of the House and says, "Mr. Speaker, I'd like to propose a bill." She or he reads the bill aloud, then drops it into the *hopper* (a special box). Then the process begins.

The Speaker sends the bill to the right *committee* (such as Armed Services). The *chairperson* of the committee sends it to the smaller part of the committee, the *subcommittee*. The members of the subcommittee hold a *hearing*, so citizens who are for and against the bill can talk. Next, members of the subcommittee get together and make changes, called *markup*. Then the subcommittee votes on the bill with its changes. If the vote is yes, the bill is sent to the entire committee for a vote. If the entire committee votes yes, the bill goes to the *Rules Committee*, which decides when different bills get voted on by the entire House of Representatives. If the majority of the House votes yes, the bill goes to the Senate, and the process starts all over again. Once the bill gets passed in both houses, it goes to the president to sign. If the president signs the bill, it becomes a *law*. If the president *vetoes* the bill, it will take two-thirds of both the House and the Senate to *override* the president's veto.

Even if the bill doesn't pass the first time, if the idea is really sound and many citizens want it, sooner or later the bill, or one similar, will probably become law. A good member of Congress continues to try to pass laws that will be fair to everyone and make our country work better.

Your Senator and Representative Work for You

Remember, even if your parents voted for the other candidate, members of Congress work for you. Congressional salaries are paid from money each wage-earner pays out in taxes. (In 1993, members of Congress earned $133,600 a year.)

Your senator or representative will have an office in your community or nearby which you may visit. If you have a question or opinion about a bill that is being considered, call or write your representative or senator. You will receive an answer.

Sometime you and your family may visit Washington, D.C. If you write to your representative or senator ahead of time to say which build-ings you would like to visit—for example, the FBI, the White House, or the Bureau of Engraving and Printing—you can get free tickets. You can also ask to meet your representative or senator. You can sit in the visitors' gallery of the House or Senate and listen to congressional debates, although, unless there is a vote scheduled, few members of Congress will be there. Most of the work of Congress gets done in committees.

Is There a Woman in the House...?

From 1789, when Congress first met, until 1916, Congress passed thousands of laws and did its various other jobs. But in all that time, no woman was ever elected to Congress. For almost the first one hundred thirty years of our country's existence, only men made the laws, which everyone—including women—had to obey. The Constitution didn't say a woman *couldn't* vote. It let each state say who was qualified. However, when the Fourteenth Amendment was ratified in 1869, giving newly freed slaves their civil rights as American citizens, it referred only to *males.* Neither black nor white women had voting rights.

In 1869, the territory of Wyoming gave women the right to vote, hold office, and serve on juries. No other territory or state had ever done this. Over the next fifty years, a few states, including Montana, gave women the vote. Finally, in 1920, the Nineteenth Amendment, granting every American woman *suffrage* (the right to vote), was ratified.

In 1916, Jeannette Rankin of Montana became the first woman elected to Congress. Although many women have since tried to get elected, until recently, they have found it very difficult. Between 1916 and 1988, only one hundred twenty-eight women served in Congress. Forty-six were either appointed by the governors of their states or elected to replace their husbands, who had died in office. One woman replaced her father. Others were appointed by the governors of their states to "hold onto" the congressional seat after the death of a congressman. They were to "keep it warm" until a special election could be held to find the right man. That is how eighty-seven-year-old Rebecca Felton became the first woman in the Senate. In 1922, the governor of Georgia appointed her to hold a seat until the male replacement could get to Washington. But Mrs. Felton insisted on being sworn in anyway. The very next day, she was replaced by the governor's man!

Many women who followed their husbands into Congress worked hard. Still, most men, among them party leaders, believed Congress should be for men only.

Elections to Congress in 1992 resulted in forty-eight women in the House (11 percent of its members) and six in the Senate (6 percent of its members). This is the largest number of women ever to serve at the same time. Yet women make up more than half the population of our country! Will women ever make up 50 percent of Congress? It will take a very long time, perhaps, but the more members of Congress who reflect the variety and interests of American citizens, the better served we will all be in our pursuit of the blessings of liberty and justice.

Jeannette, about 1903.

JEANNETTE RANKIN
First Woman in Congress

REPUBLICAN OF MONTANA
United States Representative: March 1917–March 1919; January 1941–January 1943

"Go! Go! Go! It makes no difference where! Remember, at the first opportunity, GO!" wrote Jeannette Rankin in her diary. The year was 1902, and she'd just graduated from the University of Montana. Perhaps she could feel the new century calling out to her to do something special with her life. But what?

Young women were expected to get married and raise large families. This wasn't Jeannette's idea of a modern twentieth-century woman's life. She'd already turned down two offers of marriage. And as for children, Jeannette, the oldest daughter in the family, had been like a second mother to her younger brother and sisters.

Jeannette grew up in Montana, then still a territory. Her father had come there from Canada in 1869 to prospect for gold, but he didn't find any. He turned to carpentry and ranching instead. In 1879, John Rankin married Olive Pickering, who had come from New Hampshire to teach school. Jeannette was born on June 11, 1880, nine years before Montana became a state. She was followed by Philena, who died young, then Harriet, Wellington (the only boy), Mary, Grace, and Edna.

Although the family loved the ranch, the harsh Montana winters made living on it year-round too difficult. The house was drafty and hard to heat, and there were no indoor toilets or running water. In 1885,

John Rankin built a fine house six miles away in Missoula. It was the first one in the territory to have indoor plumbing and central heating. Each summer, however, John packed up the family and headed for the ranch. Jeannette liked this. The ranch was her "thinking place." She could go off by herself, ride horses, swim, pitch hay, garden, and observe all kinds of creatures.

Of course, as did most girls, Jeannette had to learn all of the feminine arts: cooking, preserving foods, sewing, cleaning, and ironing. She was best at sewing. Once when a horse came back to the stable with its shoulder torn and bleeding, Jeannette ran for her sewing basket and a bucket of hot, soapy water. While astonished ranch hands held the horse, the ten-year-old girl cleaned the wound and neatly sewed up the animal's torn skin!

Philena (top), Harriet (left), and Jeannette (right), about 1889.

Jeannette graduated from the University of Montana in 1902 with a degree in science. But there were few jobs open to women. She tried schoolteaching ("awful"), dressmaking, for which she had a real talent ("boring"), and even furniture making ("frustrating"). So she stayed at home, reading and helping her mother with the younger children.

At twenty-eight, she left Montana to live on her own. This was a very daring thing to do. A single "lady" was supposed to stay home until she married. But her father had died and left her an allowance of seventy-five dollars a month in his will. This allowed her to be independent. Now Jeannette decided it was time to "get up and go."

Her first stop was San Francisco, where she volunteered at a settlement house on Telegraph Hill. Settlement houses were the first community centers in crowded, poorer parts of large cities. People who worked there set up clubs for children after school, taught English to the foreign-born, and tried to help people with their problems. Jeannette's experience working with poor immigrants made her think she might like to become a social worker. She traveled to New York City to enroll in the New York School of Philanthropy, the center for training social workers. Many of her teachers and fellow students were dedicated to improving the lives of workers, especially working women and children.

At that time, few states had laws to prevent children from working in factories or coal mines or from working all day at home, sewing or making cigars. Many factories lacked fire escapes or ventilation. Rarely did workers have rest periods, sick leave, or vacation time—things we now take for granted.

Life was especially difficult for working women and often hard for those women at home as well. Women could be at the mercy of cruel fathers or husbands. Most women could not vote, and often the law did not protect them. In fact, in most states, married women were forbidden by law to keep the money they earned or to own property even if they had inherited it. In twenty-three states, it was legal for a husband to give away the baby as soon as his wife gave birth!

While training to be a social worker, Jeannette visited tenement buildings in New York City. She often found entire families working for low pay in dark, cramped apartments. It was her job to try to get the younger children into school. But too often the families needed every penny the children earned.

Jeannette also went to factories where children as young as eight worked ten hours a day. She brought her information back to the classroom, where it was discussed. By the time she completed her studies, Jeannette was convinced that if women could vote, it would be possible to pass laws to make life better for women and children. (Only four states—Wyoming, Utah, Idaho, and Colorado—had thus far granted women the right to vote.)

It was a small ad in a Seattle, Washington, newspaper that changed Jeannette Rankin's life. The ad called for volunteers to put up posters asking the male citizens of Washington state to vote for woman suffrage; that is, to give women the right to vote. Jeannette, who had just moved to the state of Washington, went to the woman suffrage office in Seattle and was immediately assigned a task. She was given a stack of posters to display wherever men gathered—in restaurants, bars, stores, and barber shops. While passing out posters sounds easy, many women were unsuccessful because they were either too shy or too easily frightened by unfriendly shopkeepers.

Jeannette had a warm smile and a special way with people. Her experiences in New York had given her confidence. She had a natural ability to listen to other people, and she showed respect for all viewpoints. Even when she entered a barber shop, a place where no woman was welcome, she was allowed to leave her posters. Soon Jeannette was one of several women chosen to travel all over the state giving speeches on behalf of woman suffrage. The women's hard work paid off. On November 3, 1910, the state of Washington gave women the vote.

Next, Jeannette met with the suffragists in Missoula when she came home at Christmas. She learned that the Montana State Assembly was going to take up the issue of woman suffrage right after the new year.

The suffragists asked Jeannette to speak to the lawmakers. It would be an important speech, for no woman had ever before addressed the state assembly.

The day she spoke, the assembly chamber was decorated with flowers in honor of "the ladies." The gallery was filled with women supporters. Jeannette dressed carefully for the occasion. She wore a dark green velvet dress, and her luxurious brown hair peeked out from under a stylish, wide-brimmed hat.

Men who came to laugh were surprised. Many thought that all suffragists were dowdy old women who only wanted to do things men did because they weren't feminine.

Miss Jeannette Rankin changed their minds.

Jeannette was nervous. In order to have a moment to calm herself, she said in a clear, firm voice, "I was born in the state of Montana."

The audience went wild with applause. Her confidence returned. She explained that if Montana allowed women to vote, it would not only benefit poor women and children there but also encourage other states to follow Montana's lead. She described some of the awful conditions poor women and children were experiencing.

"It is not for myself that I am making this appeal, but for the six million women who are suffering for better conditions, women who should be working amid more sanitary conditions, under better moral conditions, at equal wages with men for equal work performed. For those women and their children, I ask that you support this measure."

But when the assembly voted, it was two votes short of the necessary two-thirds majority to place the issue on the November ballot. The women would have to try again.

The news of Jeannette's excellent speech had reached the National American Woman Suffrage Association headquarters in New York City. She was offered a job as the group's field secretary in California, where woman suffrage would soon be put to a vote. Her special task was to organize women to speak to the men in rural areas. Jeannette and her group must have been especially convincing. Even though there was a strong vote in the cities against the women, the rural areas in California carried the day. In 1911, California granted suffrage to women.

Jeannette Rankin and the other suffragists didn't always win. The antisuffragist forces beat them in several states.

Why was it so difficult for women to get the vote? Some men thought that if women voted, they wouldn't stay home and take care of the house and the children. Many men believed women weren't smart enough to vote, or that women weren't supposed to think about politics. One Harvard University professor claimed that if women were allowed to talk about politics and vote, their health would be endangered! It was very difficult to change the minds of such people. But the women didn't give up easily.

By 1914, the suffragists in Montana had convinced the state legislature to put woman suffrage on the ballot for the voters to decide. Jeannette was determined to do her part for her home state. She rushed back from her work in North Dakota to help in the campaign.

Jeannette crisscrossed the state, making speeches anywhere people would listen. She went to twenty-five towns in twenty-five days and made twenty-five speeches. Children joined their mothers in parades and on picket lines. They carried signs such as "Daddy, Please Vote 'Yes' So My Mommy Can Vote." In 1914, Montana became the tenth state to grant suffrage to women.

Several important laws were passed in Montana because women had the vote. Among them were the eight-hour workday for women (until then women and men worked twelve or even fourteen hours a day); the Lazy Husband Act, which made it a crime if a husband did not work and support his family; the Abandonment Law, which made abandoning (leaving) one's wife and children a serious crime; and a Worker's Compensation Act, which ensured that if a worker was hurt on the job, he or she would be paid by the employer while recovering and would not lose the job.

In 1916, Jeannette Rankin decided to run for the House of Representatives. Although several women had run before in other states, none had been elected. Jeannette had special advantages. Because of the work she had done on behalf of suffrage, she was well known throughout Montana. And women there, who had just won the right to vote, were eager to work on her campaign.

Jeannette wanted to serve in Congress for many reasons. She wanted to get an amendment (an addition) to the Constitution passed, giving all women in every state the right to vote, for she and other suffragists saw that it would take many years to get each state to give women the vote. She wanted to improve the conditions of women and children in the workplace throughout the country. And she wanted to prevent war. Jeannette was alarmed because war was being waged in Europe. England and France wanted the United States to join them in their fight against Germany. Despite President Woodrow Wilson's promise to keep America out of the war, people were worried. And the people of Montana didn't want to go to war.

Jeannette Rankin was a pacifist, someone who is against all wars and violence of any kind. As did many thoughtful people, she believed that if only world leaders would sit down at a conference table and talk to one another, they could settle their differences. She also believed that women were by nature peacemakers, and if given suffrage, would never vote for members of Congress who wanted war.

Jeannette had to compete with seven men running for the two Montana seats in the United States House of Representatives. She ran as a Republican, perhaps because her brother, Wellington, was a hard-working member of the Republican party. Wellington managed her campaign.

The newly enfranchised (voting) women of Montana had formed "good government clubs" all over the state, and they held teas and talks for Jeannette. She visited as many little towns and villages as she could—sometimes by train or car, and even on horseback.

On election day in November 1916, Jeannette voted and went home to wait. There was no quick way to count the votes. It could take days before the people knew who had won.

Yet, the next day, the Missoula newspapers claimed that Jeannette had lost. But two days later, Jeannette Rankin learned she'd won by more than seven thousand votes. Jeannette Rankin became the first woman elected to the Congress of the United States of America!

Not only were the citizens of Montana excited, but people all over the country were agog. What did Jeannette Rankin look like? Was it legal for a woman to be a "congressman"? Many people were thrilled by her election. Others were not.

One angry man wrote a letter to the *New York Times*. He quoted the Constitution of the United States: "No person shall be a Representative who shall not have attained to the age of twenty-five years and been seven years a citizen of the United States." He claimed that the word *person* meant a man and not a woman!

Jeannette was too busy to pay attention to such criticism. Wellington had arranged a nationwide speaking tour for her. People wanted to hear what the first woman ever elected to Congress had to say. Everywhere Jeannette went, people asked if she would vote for war. But she decided to remain silent on that topic. She wanted to speak about a constitutional amendment granting all women the right to vote, an eight-hour work-day for women and men, prohibition (that is, a law against the making and selling of all alcoholic drinks), and laws to protect children. Besides, Jeannette believed that President Woodrow Wilson meant what he said about keeping America out of war. However, the president was about to change his mind.

Jeannette's speaking tour ended when President Wilson called a special session of Congress for April 2, 1917. British intelligence agents had learned and passed on terrible news. Germany was plotting to get Mexico to enter a war against the United States. Then, German submarines sank three American ships. It appeared that Germany was looking for a fight. Even those who were against going to war were angry enough to support the president when he asked Congress to declare war.

Jeannette was deeply troubled. Before she was elected, the people of

Montana had told her they didn't want a war. But now many seemed to have changed their minds. As their representative, Jeannette wanted to do the right thing. She knew that she spoke not only for the women and men of Montana, but for *all* American women. And Jeannette believed that women should be on the side of peace. But even the suffragists were divided. Some wanted the first woman in Congress to be just like the men and not stand out. Others felt Jeannette should vote against the war. Her brother, Wellington, was urging her to vote "a man's vote" for war. Jeannette promised Wellington that she would listen carefully to all the arguments and only then would she make up her mind.

The day Jeannette Rankin arrived in Washington, D.C., thousands of women lined the streets along Pennsylvania Avenue and cheered as she was driven to the Capitol in a flag-bedecked car.

Jeannette (with shovel) plants a tree on the Capitol lawn in 1917.

Jeannette entered the House of Representatives carrying a bouquet of flowers. John Evans, her elderly Montana colleague, led her to her place. The one hundred congressmen who were already in the room stood and applauded her.

When the roll was called and her name read, a thunderous cheer went up. Congresswoman Jeannette Rankin stood and acknowledged the tribute. But after President Wilson's speech, she returned to her apartment, troubled and heartsick.

The next few days were full of anguish. Now the mood of the country favored war. On April 4, the Senate voted eighty-two in favor of war and six against, with eight not voting.

The House of Representatives scheduled its debate for April 5. At 3:18 on the morning of April 6, 1917, after sixteen hours of debate, the House was ready to vote.

The clerk began the roll call. Each representative present was to say "yes," "no," or "abstain" (not voting). When the clerk reached the "R's," Jeannette did not answer. Representative Joe Cannon rushed to her side. He whispered, "Little woman, you cannot afford not to vote. You represent the womanhood of the country in the American Congress." But Jeannette knew that there would be a second roll call.

"Rankin, Rankin," the clerk called out once again. Jeannette stood up. She gripped the back of the seat in front of her. "I want to stand by my country," she said slowly, "but I cannot vote for war. I vote 'no.'"

But the House voted overwhelmingly to join the conflict, with three hundred seventy-four in favor, fifty opposed, and nine abstentions. The United States was at war.

Although fifty members of the House had voted against war, it was Jeannette's "no" that seemed to matter. The *New York Times* declared that her vote "was final proof of feminine incapacity for straight reasoning." A magazine called the *Nation* warned that allowing women to vote wasn't such a good idea after all. Wellington was furious. "You've lost your chance to ever get reelected," he argued. Many of Jeannette's friends from the suffrage movement felt she had let them down.

But Jeannette said, "I don't care what people think about me now. It matters what people will think about me in fifty years from now." And she went to work introducing legislation to help make the lives of women and children easier.

Her first success was an amendment to a bill in which she asked the federal government to employ more skilled women. Next, she introduced a bill to establish a program of women's health education. Both became law. Some bills she worked on failed, such as one which would have given special allowances to families of men who were fighting the war.

Jeannette, along with other members of Congress, created a special suffrage committee. Its job was to write an amendment to the Constitution that would give all women who were American citizens and at least twenty-one years of age the right to vote. She served on that committee. But it wasn't until 1920, after Jeannette had left office, that the Nineteenth Amendment to the Constitution granted women the vote.

Each day, Jeannette received dozens of visitors from all over the country. Almost everyone wanted a personal glimpse of the first woman in Congress. One day a young woman from Missoula came to see her. Her sister was employed by the Bureau of Engraving and Printing, which manufactured paper money, war bonds, and postage stamps. She complained that the women workers were forced to work twelve- and fourteen-hour shifts even though women who worked for the government had won the right to work an eight-hour day. They were not permitted to take rest breaks and had only half an hour in which to eat their meal. All sick days and vacation time had been cancelled.

The next day, Jeannette paid a visit to the bureau. She noted that although the rooms in which the women worked were well lit, those who inspected the money had to stand on their feet for the entire working day. Others had to lift heavy packages of paper.

Jeannette hired a private investigator from New York City to take down the women's complaints. Then Jeannette confronted the director, Joseph Ralph, with the evidence. He was annoyed that Jeannette questioned his decisions. Next, Jeannette Rankin went directly to Ralph's boss, Secretary of the Treasury William G. McAdoo. When she said she would order a congressional investigation if the eight-hour day was not restored in one week, Mr. McAdoo's assistant shook his finger at her and said the government didn't work that way. But Jeannette was firm. She repeated her demand and her threat of an investigation. That evening, Mr. McAdoo announced the return of the eight-hour day as well as an investigation of conditions at the bureau. Within days, the women were granted vacations, regular rest periods, only a half-day's work on Saturday—and a new director. Soon several hundred new workers were hired. Jeannette got a law passed increasing the wages paid to the women. (The men had already been offered a raise.)

But Jeannette Rankin was defeated when she ran for Congress in 1918. All of her valuable work for women could not overcome the anger the citizens of Montana felt towards her single vote cast against the war.

If she was disappointed, Jeannette didn't show it. She devoted herself to finding a way to ensure world peace. She worked for the National Council for Prevention of War, the Women's International League for Peace and Freedom, and other pacifist groups. In 1923, she bought a plot of land in the state of Georgia. She hoped to create a model community where people could plan for a world without war. In 1935, her Georgia farmhouse burned to the ground. Soon after, she returned to Montana.

In 1940, when she was sixty years old, the United States was once again on the brink of war. And once again, the people of Montana chose Jeannette Rankin to be a member of the House of Representatives. Jeannette ran on a peace platform.

On December 7, 1941, the Japanese attacked Pearl Harbor, an American naval base in Hawaii. This time there was no long debate in Congress when President Roosevelt asked for a vote to go to war. In less

Jeannette seals a letter to President Nixon in 1971, asking him to end the Vietnam War.

than one hour, both the Senate and the House of Representatives voted yes. This time the only member of the House or Senate to vote against the war was Congresswoman Jeannette Rankin.

Many people begged her to change her mind, but Jeannette Rankin remained true to her belief that war was not the way to settle disputes between nations.

Jeannette Rankin served out her second term in Congress, and retired from politics, but not from her peace activities. Wherever people protested against war, she joined them. At the age of eighty-eight, she led a group of five thousand women, known as the Jeannette Rankin Brigade, down Pennsylvania Avenue to the steps of the Capitol to protest the war in Vietnam. It was the very same route on which she had so triumphantly traveled to take her place in Congress.

She died in 1973, just before her ninety-third birthday.

Senator Smith at her desk in 1942.

MARGARET CHASE SMITH:
A Woman of Conscience

REPUBLICAN OF MAINE
United States Representative: June 1940–January 1949
United States Senator: January 1949–January 1973

Margaret Madeline Chase's first trip to Washington, D.C., was in 1916 with her high school's senior class. The trip lasted ten days, and it cost sixty dollars. That was a lot of money for a teenager to save, but Margaret had been earning her own spending money ever since she was thirteen. The most remarkable event of that trip was that she got to shake hands with President Woodrow Wilson. Margaret did not imagine that she herself would one day become an important member of Congress and a candidate for the office of president, and that five more presidents would eagerly shake *her* hand during her thirty-three-year career as a public servant.

Margaret was born in Skowhegan, Maine, on December 14, 1897. Situated on the Kennebec River, Skowhegan is a small industrial town, once known for its textiles and later for the manufacture of shoes. She was the oldest of six children, three boys and three girls. They were all born in the same green-shuttered house her grandfather had built when he was a young man.

Margaret's father was a barber. When times were hard, her mother worked as a clerk in Green Brothers' Five and Ten Cent Store. Margaret couldn't wait until she was old enough to work, too. When she was twelve, she asked the manager of Green's for a job. "Can you reach that top shelf?" he replied. Margaret couldn't. So the manager said kindly,

Margaret in 1903 at the age of six.
Courtesy of Margaret Chase Smith.

"When you can reach that top shelf, you can come back, and I'll talk seriously with you."

Exactly one year later, Margaret returned to remind the manager of his promise. "Can you reach that top shelf?" he asked again. Now, standing on her tiptoes, she just made it. "Come in on Saturday nights from six until ten," the manager said.

Margaret was paid fifty cents for the four hours. During Christmas vacation, she worked for a whole week and earned thirty dollars. She was thrilled. "I was always independent. I just didn't like to take money from my parents, with all of the other children needing things."

Her good work habits were noticed by many customers, including the woman who ran the telephone company. She offered to teach Margaret to be an operator. The young girl learned quickly and soon took over the night shift. Since there weren't many telephones in Skowhegan in the early 1900s, there wasn't much to do at night. Margaret could finish her schoolwork and get some sleep on the cot that was kept next to the switchboard. Many years later, at age ninety-three, Margaret Chase Smith could still remember some of those telephone numbers: "Thirty-one was the insurance man; five hundred nineteen, the town office."

Margaret always loved sports, and in her senior year of high school she coached the girls' basketball team. She had dreams of becoming an athletic coach, but she never seemed to have enough tuition money for college. "Every time I got a little money saved, I'd have to have a new pair of shoes or something," she recalled. Yet even without a college degree, she was offered a job teaching in a one-room schoolhouse in a nearby village. There were twelve students. She taught there for two years.

After her teaching job ended, she worked for the local weekly newspaper and soon became known as "a girl about town" because she was aware of everything happening in Skowhegan. A few years later, the owner of the woolen mill asked her to be his office manager. Margaret's salary jumped from twenty-eight dollars a week at the newspaper to more than one hundred dollars a week at the mill.

With the higher pay came much more responsibility. For the first six months, Margaret went home and cried every night because she knew that if anyone in the office made a mistake, she would be held accountable. "But then," she said, "I got hold of it."

It was love and marriage that took Margaret away from the mill. In 1930, Margaret Madeline Chase married Clyde H. Smith, a wealthy newspaper owner and Republican politician. "And after that, I worked even harder," she said.

In 1936, Clyde decided to run for governor of Maine. But because of an inner party struggle, another man got the nomination. Clyde ran for Congress instead. That was a fateful decision. If Clyde Smith hadn't become a congressman, Margaret Chase Smith might never have had the opportunity to serve in Congress.

Margaret worked diligently to get Clyde elected. She gave speeches, wrote his letters, answered his phone calls, and held gala parties. Her years as a businesswoman gave her the confidence to organize his campaign. Whatever had to be done, she did quickly and efficiently—and without pay.

When Clyde won and the couple went to Washington, the new congressman expected Margaret to work in his office for free, even though every member of the House and Senate has a budget to hire staff. But Clyde hadn't counted on Margaret's independence and strong will.

Margaret held out for a paycheck. Clyde finally gave in and paid her a salary. She organized his office as efficiently as she had organized her boss's office at the woolen mill.

After two terms in the House of Representatives, Clyde Smith was preparing to run again when he suffered a serious heart attack. Margaret was hosting a huge party for her husband's campaign at the state Republican convention in Portland, Maine. She hurried back to Washington and found the doctor very worried. He warned Clyde not to run for office again and urged Margaret to take his place. Clyde agreed. He dictated a letter to the Maine Republican Committee requesting that the name of Margaret Chase Smith replace his on the Republican party's primary ballot. (A primary election is held by a political party when more than one person wants to be the party's candidate. Only voters who belong to that party—in this case, the Republicans of Maine—get to choose the candidate they like best. The winner runs against the candi-

Margaret and Clyde in 1936.

dates of the other parties in the general election.)

Margaret typed the letter, Clyde signed it, and it was witnessed by the doctor and a nurse. Then Margaret sent copies to the newspapers and to the Republican Committee in Maine.

Before the newspapers hit the stands the next morning, Clyde Smith was dead. Margaret was stunned and grief-stricken. Theirs had been a close, loving marriage. Margaret was Clyde's helpmate and most trusted friend. She felt certain that if she had been elected to Congress, they would still have worked in much the same way as when Clyde was the congressman and she his aide. The only difference would have been that he would have helped her and conserved his strength.

Now, however, Margaret was on her own. Despite her grief, she decided to stand for election in Clyde's place, for that was what he had wanted. It was now the beginning of April 1940. Margaret had an enormous task ahead. First she had to run in a primary and a regular election in June just to be able to finish out her husband's current term in

Congress. Then she had to run in a second primary election, also in June, in order to be the Republican candidate for Congress in the general election that fall.

Some Republican leaders in Maine weren't happy that Margaret Chase Smith was going to stay in the race. Several Republican men who wanted to be in Congress ran against her in both primaries.

But Margaret Chase Smith trounced her opponents in all four elections (the Republicans in the primaries and the Democrats in the general elections). She became one of just seven women in the House of Representatives.

Her first task was to get appointed to the committee where she could do the most good for the people of Maine.

Most of the important work done by members of Congress goes on in committees, because it would be too difficult for each member of Congress to study every issue. By serving on just a few committees, a member of Congress can become an expert on certain issues, such as veterans' affairs or agriculture. In the House of Representatives there are twenty-two "standing," or permanent, committees. In the Senate there are sixteen. Members of Congress always want to be on at least one committee whose work will benefit the people back home.

With World War II already underway in Europe and the Far East, Margaret wanted to be sure our country had a strong navy. This would be good for the nation and good for Maine. Not only was Maine a shipbuilding state, but it had a long coastline on the Atlantic Ocean. Many people feared it could be attacked by Germany if America entered the war. Margaret wanted to serve on the Naval Affairs Committee. She convinced the chairman to assign her to it, even though he thought only men should be concerned with naval affairs. (Later Margaret served on its successor, the Armed Services Committee.) One of the laws she helped write provided more money to strengthen the navy.

When Margaret made an official trip to a base in Hawaii in 1941 to see how well the navy was operating, she made a disturbing discovery. The nurses who cared for sick and wounded sailors were not considered part

President Truman signs a law granting military women new rights.

of the navy, even though they were on active duty! Women could only belong to the Naval Reserves. This meant that unless there was a national emergency, the women would only get paid when they were on duty. Unlike the men, women had no job security. If they became ill on active duty, they were simply sent home and lost their navy jobs.

Margaret was outraged. She believed that "women ought to take their place as people and be recognized for their ability." When she returned to Washington, she went to the secretary of the navy and said, "If nurses are important, they should receive the same benefits as navy men. And if the navy doesn't need them, the women shouldn't be there."

It would be several years before Margaret convinced Congress to pass laws to make women full-fledged members of the military. Finally, in 1948, after World War II was over and thousands of women had served with honor, President Harry S. Truman signed a bill into law giving all military women some important rights. They were made part of the regular armed services, paid the same salaries as men, and given the same benefits. Still, there were some things military women weren't permitted: no woman could be ranked higher than colonel; women weren't allowed to serve on ships; and they were not allowed in combat. (Over the years, changes have been made giving military women more equality with military men.)

"The Lady from Maine," as Margaret was affectionately called, made news wherever she went. In her early years as a member of the House of Representatives, what she ate or wore or said was reported in her hometown newspaper, throughout the state of Maine, and even around the country. She became known for pinning a single fresh red rose on her dress or suit jacket every day and for wearing two strands of pearls around her neck. When she admitted a fondness for cream-cheese-and-green-olive sandwiches, which she ate at her desk at lunchtime, women all over America ate them for lunch, too.

By her own reckoning, Margaret Chase Smith voted the same way as her fellow Republicans did 96 percent of the time. But her independent nature would not allow her to go along with her political party if she disagreed with its views. For example, she voted in favor of the United States becoming part of the United Nations, something many Republicans were against. When Margaret voted to help the war-torn countries of Europe after World War II by loaning them large sums of money, many Republicans were angry with her. They didn't want the taxpayers' money spent that way. But Margaret believed it was important to help rebuild Europe.

In 1948, after she had served four terms in the House of Representatives, one of the two senators from Maine retired. Margaret decided to run for the Senate. With her eight years of service in the House, Margaret believed that she was the best-qualified person for the job.

Once again, as in 1940 when Margaret wanted to be the Republican nominee for the House, there would be a spirited fight among the Maine Republicans. Three male contenders entered the Republican primary, hoping to be selected as the candidate.

Two of the men were honorable. One was not. He tried to turn the voters away from Margaret by "smearing" her good name and her character. He accused her of being sympathetic to the Soviet Union and the Communists.

During this time in our history, many Americans feared the Soviet Union. They believed Soviet leaders wanted to take over the United States by force and change our democratic form of government to a Communist one. It seemed as if the world were divided into allies of the United States and allies of the Soviets. Communism appealed to many people in the world because its leaders promised that one day it would be possible for each person to have what he or she needed to live a comfortable life. This would happen only if factories, farms, and homes were owned by the government. But the rulers of the Soviet Union would allow only one political party and would not permit their citizens to criticize their leaders. The punishment for disagreement could be prison or even death.

Few Americans ever believed in the Soviet system of government or were members of the Communist party. But many Americans were afraid of communism. They thought that any person who complained about how things were done in America was a Communist and a traitor to our country. However, the First Amendment to our Constitution gives people the right to criticize our government. It is a freedom that the founders of our country cherished and passed on to future generations.

The man who wanted Margaret's place on the Republican ticket told the voters that she was not a patriot. He said that on one hundred seven occasions, Margaret had voted the same way as a congressman from New York City whom some people called a Communist.

Margaret was furious. At first she wanted to answer the charges against her. The record showed that fifteen other Republicans had voted the same way she had on each of those issues. But only she was being attacked.

However, her good friend and adviser, Bill Lewis, told her to wait. He reasoned that if Margaret answered those charges right away, the man would say other untrue things about her. Margaret listened to that advice. She campaigned on her record as a congresswoman who had always worked hard for her country and for the state of Maine.

Then in May, just three weeks before the primary election, Margaret spoke before a Republican women's club in Skowhegan and strongly defended her record. She challenged each of the false things her opponent had said about her, proving him wrong on every count.

Reporters from many newspapers were taking notes, and the next day, her speech made the front pages. Editors from across the state of Maine praised Margaret Chase Smith for standing up to the person who had attacked her record. She easily won the primary, and in the 1948 general election, she beat her Democratic rival by sixty-three thousand votes. Margaret Chase Smith became the first woman ever elected to both the House and the Senate.

Over the next few years, the fear of communism grew stronger in America. Communism had taken hold in China, North Korea, and other countries. The United States was fighting alongside the South Koreans to stop communism from spreading further. At home, Alger Hiss, a man who worked for the State Department, was convicted of lying to a congressional committee about having passed secrets to the Russians.

In 1950, a senator from Wisconsin, Joseph R. McCarthy, made a speech in Wheeling, West Virginia. As he spoke, he held up a piece of paper and waved it at the audience. He claimed the two hundred seven names on that paper were those of Communist supporters who worked for the U.S. State Department.

This speech frightened Americans. Many accusations and investigations followed. Senator McCarthy used the Senate floor to accuse hundreds of people of being Communists or knowing those who were Communists. He accused people who taught in our colleges and universities or wrote or acted in the theater, radio, or the movies, as well as those who worked for our government. Many men and women lost their jobs because Senator McCarthy or his friends called them Communists or said they knew someone who was a Communist. The accused people were powerless to fight back, because while conducting their official work, members of Congress can speak without fear of being sued for slander (damage to a person's reputation).

At first Senator Smith thought Senator McCarthy was onto something important. She thought communism did pose a threat to our country. If what McCarthy said were true, then there might be hundreds, perhaps even thousands, of secret Communists spying on the United States. Certainly Congress needed to investigate. So, every time Senator McCarthy made a speech about Communists in the government, Margaret listened carefully.

She became suspicious, however, when Senator McCarthy never produced any proof. She began to suspect he was a dangerous man who should be stopped from unjust attacks on people. Margaret knew that if she publicly criticized him, some would accuse *her* of being a Communist. Her career as a senator might end. But her independence and honesty would not allow her to keep quiet.

At the end of May 1950, Margaret wrote a statement that became known as a "Declaration of Conscience." Then she contacted six other Republican senators who read her paper and signed it. This act took a great deal of courage. Almost every member of Congress feared Senator McCarthy.

The next day Margaret left the Senate Office Building and took the little subway train over to the Capitol. She and Joe McCarthy were the only two people on it. He sat beside her.

"You look pretty gloomy," Senator McCarthy said. "What's going on?"

"I'm going to make a speech, and you're not going to like it," she answered.

When the train stopped, he dashed into the Senate and sat down.

At noon on June 1, Margaret rose to speak before the Senate. "I think that it is high time that we remembered that the Constitution speaks . . . not only of the freedom of speech but also of trial by jury instead of trial by accusation."

She warned that people who accuse others without proof ignore basic American rights: "the right to criticize; the right to hold unpopular beliefs; the right to protest; and the right of independent thought." She said those who accuse others falsely were using the tools of dictators. If allowed to go on, such actions could destroy the American way of life.

When she finished her speech, Senator McCarthy rushed angrily from the room.

Some newspapers attacked Senator Smith for being too critical of Senator McCarthy. But in Maine, about 80 percent of the people supported her. Most members of Congress, however, were still afraid to speak out. Even President Harry S. Truman did not criticize McCarthy in public, although he later told Margaret that hers "was one of the greatest speeches and most needed of anything I've seen."

Finally, in 1954, the full Senate voted to censure (officially criticize) the senator from Wisconsin. The McCarthy era was over. But Margaret was still concerned about communism. That same year she voted to outlaw the Communist Party. In 1968, she voted to appropriate money to support the Communist Subversive Activity Control Board.

Margaret Chase Smith was reelected to the Senate for three more terms. During that time she voted her Republican conscience. She worried that Americans were losing their family values. From 1966 to 1970, she sponsored several bills to make the film industry put ratings on each movie so parents would know if they were suitable for children. Her bills did not pass. She also voted for laws to fight crime, such as the "No-Knock Law," which passed in 1968. This law allowed the police, under certain circumstances, to enter a suspicious place without getting special permission from a judge.

In 1964, a group of Republican women from Chicago who weren't satisfied with the choices they were being offered asked Margaret if she would run for president of the United States. Even though she knew she wouldn't get the nomination, she ran in several presidential primaries. Margaret was proud that many people thought she'd make a good president. "It showed that a woman was a person and if qualified and serious, would be given serious consideration." When a television interviewer asked how a woman president would handle other world leaders, she replied that "a woman president would probably do as well as Joan of Arc, Catherine the Great, and Queen Victoria." At the Republican National Convention in July, Senator George Aiken of

Margaret at the Republican National Convention in 1964.

Vermont nominated Margaret for the presidency. However, Barry Goldwater became the Republican choice. That year, a Democrat, Lyndon Baines Johnson, won the national election.

In 1972, Margaret Chase Smith's thirty-three years of public service came to a close. She was nearly seventy-five years old, and she was a bit weary. For the first time, the people of Maine voted in favor of an opponent, William Hathaway. He said that Maine needed a younger, more energetic person to represent its people.

Of course, the defeat hurt. But Margaret Chase Smith became a much-sought-after lecturer on college campuses. She set up the Margaret Chase Smith Library next to her home in Skowhegan. People come from all over the country to do research at the library. And each year, hundreds of schoolchildren come to meet her and ask questions about her extraordinary career as the first woman to serve in both the House of Representatives and the Senate, and the first woman to be nominated for the office of president of the United States at a national convention of a major political party. Most of all, people come to shake hands with a woman who had the courage to speak out against Senator Joe McCarthy, a man who tried to destroy the cherished right of all Americans to free speech and the right to challenge their accusers.

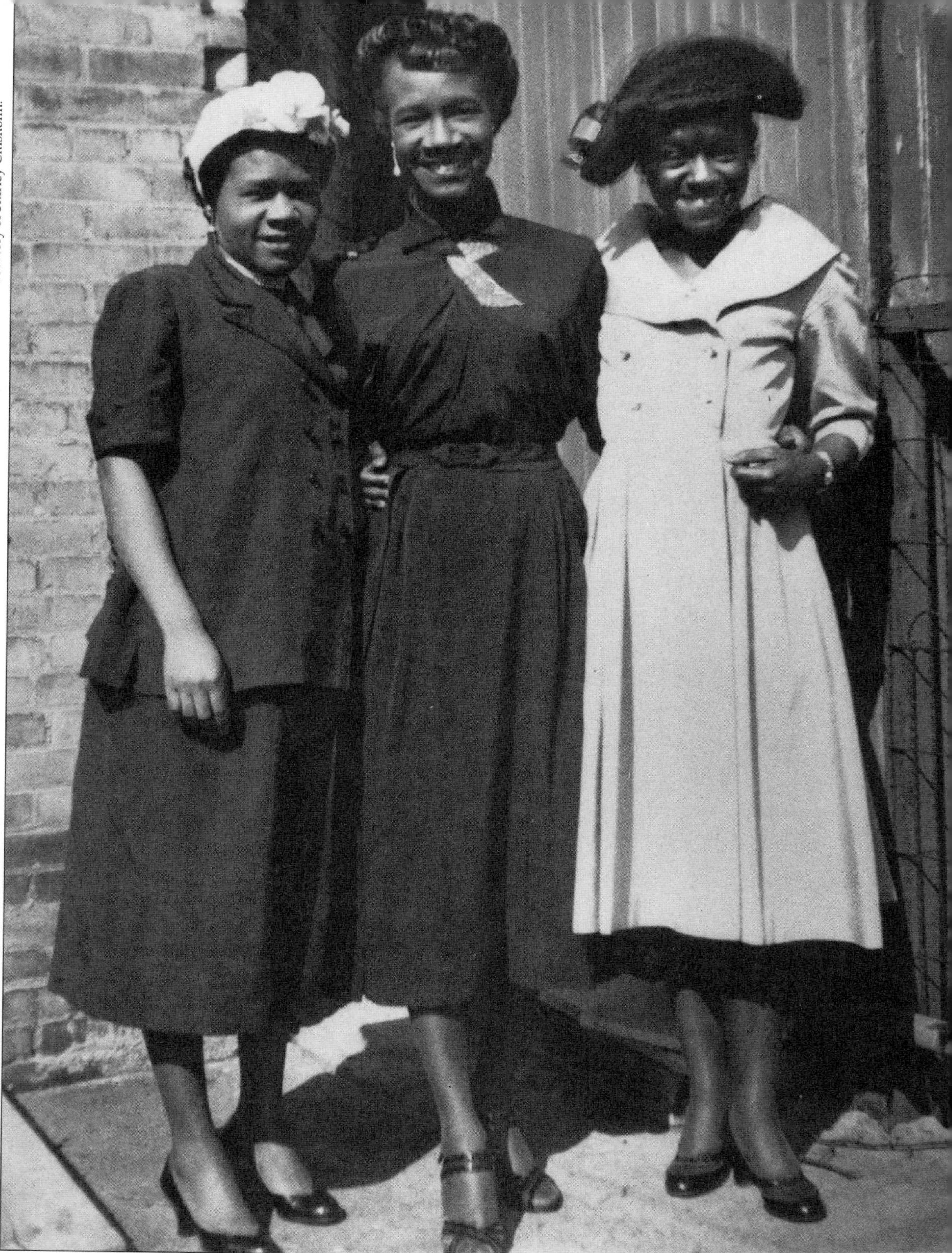

Courtesy of Shirley Chisholm.

SHIRLEY CHISHOLM

"Even Though You Are Black and a Woman, Don't Let It Stand in Your Path"

DEMOCRAT OF NEW YORK
United States Representative: January 1969–January 1983

"The most important thing for you to remember, Shirley, is that your brain power is going to make the difference in your life." These words of encouragement were spoken to eight-year-old Shirley Anita St. Hill by her grandmother. Although she now can't recall the exact reason for that lecture, Shirley never forgot those words.

Shirley Anita St. Hill was born in Brooklyn, New York, on November 30, 1924. Her parents, Ruby and Charles St. Hill, had immigrated there from the Caribbean island of Barbados in order to make a better life for themselves. The St. Hills had set two firm goals for their family: an education for their children and a home of their own.

The 1920s were boom times for many Americans. But they were not good years for black people to find well-paid jobs. The only work Charles St. Hill could get was as a baker's helper. Ruby was a seamstress, but with three little girls, the oldest of whom was three, she couldn't go out to work.

The St. Hills made a very difficult decision. Because they could not feed the family of five on Charles's tiny paycheck plus the small amount Ruby earned by sewing at home, they sent Shirley and her younger sisters, Odessa and Muriel, to live in Barbados with Grandmother Seale. Mrs. St. Hill took the children to Barbados and stayed with them for six months until they settled in. She believed that within a year or two at the most, the St. Hills's fortunes would change, and the family would be reunited in Brooklyn.

Shirley (center) and her sisters Odessa (left) and Selma (right), about 1968.

But things didn't work out that way. Soon after Ruby went back to Brooklyn, she had another baby girl. Once again, she couldn't go out to work. It would be seven and a half years before Shirley and her sisters would return to Brooklyn.

However, for the St. Hill girls on Grandmother Seale's farm, it was "a wonderful life," recalled Shirley. "It was very different from the life of children who grow up in the inner city." It's true that Shirley and her sisters had many chores to do. One was to draw dozens of buckets of water from the well each day. But there were endless things to learn and enjoy on the farm as well as delicious fruits and vegetables to be had for the picking. And there were the beautiful blue waters of the Caribbean nearby. The girls went swimming almost every day.

When it was time for Shirley to attend the village school, she learned to sing "God Save the King," since Barbados is part of the British Commonwealth.

What a wrench it was for Shirley, at ten, to suddenly land back in her old Brooklyn neighborhood. Of course, it was wonderful to be reunited with her mom and dad and to meet her new little sister, Selma. But it was hard for Shirley to navigate the strange streets with their tall, dingy buildings and hordes of unfamiliar people.

If her mother sent her on an errand, Shirley would invariably get lost. "My mother told me I had to learn to read street signs so I'd know where I was going." She was used to looking for landmarks, such as a shoe-maker's shop. In Barbados, shops stayed where they were for generations. In Brooklyn, it seemed to Shirley, stores closed down and new ones sprang up almost overnight. Fortunately, the police station stayed put. Often a kind policeman brought a lost Shirley back home.

Shirley was almost eleven when she enrolled in the neighborhood ele-mentary school. She expected to be a sixth grader. Her math and English were superior, and she had a large vocabulary. However, she didn't know any American history or geography. In Barbados, she had learned British history and geography. She was sent down to the third grade.

Shirley was humiliated. She always finished her lessons quickly.

Then she set out to make trouble. "I was bored, and so I learned to make the best spitballs in the school, and I had a marvelous time." Fortunately, a wise teacher recognized what was wrong. She saw to it that Shirley was skipped up to sixth grade and given a tutor. Within a few months, Shirley had caught up. Afterwards, she was always at the top of her class.

The most troubling thing Shirley encountered in Brooklyn was racism. For the first time, she heard the word *nigger*. Whenever black and white children got into fights, the white children would call, "You nigger! You nigger!" Then, "the black children would jump on the white kids, and they would roll around the sidewalk. That was amazing to me. It was one of the most difficult things for me to become accustomed to."

If life in Brooklyn was sometimes difficult and frightening, Shirley's relationship with her father made up for it. Although Charles St. Hill did not have a high school education, he had a curious mind and was a great reader. Every day he bought three different newspapers. He would give each child a section to read, and at dinner he would expect them to discuss what they had learned. Shirley was his most willing student.

Charles St. Hill went to meetings where African-Americans discussed their problems and how to solve them. He was a follower of Marcus Garvey, a black leader who had founded the Universal Negro Improvement Association in 1914. Marcus Garvey wanted to lead African-Americans back to Africa to form a new nation. Mr. St. Hill would take Shirley to these meetings. Afterwards, the two talked about what they'd heard. "Very few dads brought their kids along to those meetings," Shirley said. Her father's attention made her feel special.

Shirley's mother didn't think it was proper for her daughter to attend such gatherings. She would say, "Charlie, leave the child alone. Stop dragging her all over."

Her dad would answer, "Ruby, I'm not dragging her all over. She's bright. I want her to learn everything and understand. I want her to ask questions."

Shirley enjoyed these excursions with her dad, but she often chafed at her mother's strict rules. Her mother didn't want Shirley to visit with her friends. She had to come right home from school. And when her mother worked as a cleaning lady, it was Shirley's job to pick up her sisters every day at lunchtime, race home with them, make them lunch, and get everyone back to school before the bell rang. After school, she would have to bring them all straight home again. And on Sundays, the girls attended church not just once, but three times. The neighborhood children thought it was funny to see the sisters go to church so often. They would chant after them, "Here come the St. Hill girls!"

Their church did not permit dancing, and that bothered Shirley, who loved to dance. But her mother believed that Shirley's dancing would lead her into a life of sin. When Mrs. St. Hill allowed Shirley to go to a party, she would make her take all her sisters along so they could tell Shirley not to dance!

Shirley St. Hill was the first member of her family to attend college. The St. Hill dream was coming true. And before Shirley graduated, Ruby and Charles bought their own home, a three-story house on Prospect Place in Brooklyn.

Shirley entered Brooklyn College in 1942. She tried to distance herself from her mother's strong grip by spending as much time as possible on campus, coming home only to sleep. One of her favorite extracurricular activities was the debating society. Even though she lisped, she was an excellent debater. Shirley never overcame this difficulty, but she never let it become a problem when she had to give a speech. Her favorite teacher, a blind professor named Louis Warsoff, recognized her talent as a speaker and a leader. He urged Shirley to think about going into politics.

Shirley and "Proffy," as she called Warsoff, often took long walks together to discuss politics. When he wanted Shirley to run for student president, she reminded him that she was not only black but also a woman. "But Proffy would shrug it off and say, 'Yes, we know that. But you have what it takes.'" Shirley lost that election, but not by many votes.

Professor Warsoff wasn't the only one to recognize that Shirley St. Hill had ability. When she won the debating prize in 1946, it was presented to her at Brooklyn College by Eleanor Roosevelt, then ambassador to the

United Nations. Mrs. Roosevelt said, "Shirley St. Hill, even though you are black and a woman, don't let it stand in your path."

When Shirley graduated in June 1946, few careers were open to college-educated African-American women. Shirley decided to become a nursery school teacher.

It wasn't her race or her sex that almost stopped Shirley from landing her first teaching job. It was her size. Only five feet, two inches tall, and weighing ninety pounds, Shirley was turned down by school after school. Apparently teachers, even nursery school teachers, were supposed to be tall and tough-looking! "I had to beg the director of the Mt. Calvary Child Care Center in Harlem to give me a chance," she said. Shirley was sure that once she got her foot in the door, she would be a fine teacher—and she was. Then she enrolled at Columbia University's night school for a master's degree in early childhood education.

In her free time, Shirley went dancing. It was at one of these dances that she met Conrad Chisholm, an insurance investigator. In 1949, they were married. They never had children.

Shirley's career flourished. Soon she became director of a large day care center on the Lower East Side of Manhattan. Later, she was made a consultant for New York City's Division of Day Care.

But Shirley never forgot Professor Warsoff's suggestion that she ought to be in politics. And in the early 1950s, she began to volunteer at the local Democratic club in her home district. (All over the country, there are both Democratic and Republican clubs. Registered voters who wish to work for their parties join them. Clubs do many different jobs, including choosing candidates to run for mayor, city council, or state assembly; raising money for political campaigns; and providing people to help candidates research issues, put up posters, and do whatever has to be done to win elections.)

Shirley quickly became known as a troublemaker. She didn't accept the role assigned to women and African-Americans by the white men who ran the club. Even though half the population of Shirley's district was either African-American or Latino, no one from either of these groups had ever held elective office. And the women who belonged to the club were only allowed to raise money and stuff envelopes with campaign material. They never made important decisions such as who could run for political office or who was in charge of the club.

In 1961, Shirley and other minority members of the Democratic club formed their own group, the Unity club. She worked to register voters, especially blacks and Latinos, so they could vote for her candidate for the New York State Assembly. He was Tom Jones, an African-American. Because Shirley's Spanish was excellent (she had studied it in college), she was able to convince many Spanish-speaking citizens to vote for Mr. Jones. He won the election.

Two years later, when Mr. Jones was chosen to be a civil court judge, Shirley decided to run for the state assembly herself. She knew that she was qualified for the job. She would not let her race or sex stop her. Some people criticized her, saying that because she was a woman, she should stay home. But Shirley was well known in her district, and she won the election in a landslide victory.

When she arrived in Albany, the state capital, in 1964, she asked to be put on the Education Committee since she had had more than fifteen years of experience working with children. During her four years in Albany, nine of the bills she proposed were passed by the assembly. Five were then voted down in the state senate, but four were signed into law. One gave unemployment insurance coverage to domestic workers (maids and cleaning women). Shirley was especially proud of this because her mother had been a cleaning woman. Another law she sponsored created a special program to give talented minority youths money to attend college. This program was called SEEK. It stands for "Search for Education, Elevation, and Knowledge."

In 1968, Shirley decided to run for Congress although no black woman had ever been elected before. In fact, there was only one black member of Congress at that time. His name was Adam Clayton Powell, Jr., and he was from the section of New York City known as Harlem.

The Republicans saw an opportunity to gain a seat in Congress by running a well-known black civil rights leader, James Farmer, against Shirley. But Mr. Farmer didn't live in Shirley's district. He had only moved there so he could run in that election.

Mr. Farmer aimed his message at the male voters, bringing in musicians to play from the backs of sound trucks. He made fun of that "little schoolteacher" who was trying to get elected to Congress. Since New York City traditionally elects Democrats to Congress, the Republicans were anxious to win this congressional seat. They gave a lot of money to Mr. Farmer's campaign. Shirley didn't have much money. But she had spent years helping to register voters in her district, and she knew there were more women voters than men. She had their support. Her campaign slogan was "Fighting Shirley Chisholm: Unbought and Unbossed."

Shirley had shopping bags printed with her slogan. Women and children filled them with campaign literature and gave them out at subway stops and in housing projects. People in Shirley's district understood that these bags were a symbol of the African-American women who worked as cleaning women and came home each night with shopping bags filled with their work clothes and perhaps the evening meal. And the voters knew that Shirley Chisholm had fought in the

Shirley speaks to students on the steps of the Capitol, about 1977.

New York State Assembly to get these low-paid workers some of the same benefits other workers enjoyed.

Shirley campaigned in the streets and in the churches and synagogues (Jewish houses of prayer). She said she would be a good representative for all her constituents (the people in her district), regardless of race, religion, or ethnic origin.

When the election was over, Shirley Chisholm had defeated James Farmer by more than two to one. The first black woman in Congress joined just eight other women there. Within two years, four more women were elected to the House of Representatives. "There were so few of us, we stuck together," Shirley said. As a member of Congress, she found more problems connected with being a woman than with being black. "I have to say that I have met far more discrimination as a woman than as a black in politics," she noted.

At first she was assigned to the Agriculture Committee. This wasn't a good committee for a representative from Brooklyn! And when she discovered her subcommittee assignment was to be rural development and forestry, Shirley was furious. How could she do any good for her city constituents if she had to worry about forests? (Most of the work of each committee is done in smaller units called subcommittees. Members of the subcommittee consider bills in its special area. They examine all aspects of a bill to find out if it is a good one. Members of a subcommittee might call in experts to testify, for example. After the subcommittee members learn as much as possible about the pros and cons of a bill, they recommend a yes or no vote to the whole committee.)

Although the Speaker (the presiding officer) of the House told Shirley to sit back and "be a good soldier," she decided to fight the assignment. She marched up to him and demanded a different committee assignment. Her first choice was the Education and Labor Committee, but if that wasn't possible, then at least she wanted to be on a committee where she could help her constituents, many of whom were unemployed. Finally, Shirley got the Veterans' Affairs Committee. "There are a lot more veterans in my district than there are trees," she thought. In later years, she was assigned to the Education and Labor Committee, where she sponsored bills that provided scholarships and loans to help women, minority students, and older people attend college. She co-authored a bill that gave minority students access to information about special tests that students must take in order to get into college.

When Shirley came to Congress, many House members were aghast at her outspokenness, which began with her open challenge of her committee assignment. Some men warned her that "freshman" (first year) members of Congress were supposed to be quiet and listen to the more experienced members. But Shirley always said what was on her mind and fought for what she believed in, even though she didn't win all of the time. Instead of being quiet during her first term, she joined fifteen members of Congress who urged that money be cut from the defense budget. She called for an end to the war in Vietnam, and with some of her colleagues, introduced legislation to end the military draft. She called for the U.S. to stop selling arms to South Africa.

Congresswoman Chisholm fought hard for the people she represented. She understood the need of working mothers for safe day care facilities and introduced legislation to extend the hours the centers stayed open. Although this bill passed in the House and Senate, it was vetoed by the president. She sponsored the Adequate Income Act of 1971 to guarantee an annual income for all American families. That bill did not pass.

Shirley Chisholm served in the House of Representatives for fourteen years. She supported the Equal Rights Amendment (ERA), which would have been the twenty-seventh amendment to our Constitution. Although Congress passed the ERA in 1972, it didn't become part of the Constitution because only thirty-five out of the necessary thirty-eight states voted to ratify it. The ERA says men and women must be treated equally under the law. Supporters of the ERA hoped that its passage would wipe out all laws which discriminate against women because of their sex. Critics of the ERA said women were already protected by the Constitution, and the amendment wasn't necessary.

Congresswoman Chisholm also supported the right of a woman to

Shirley at a rally for Democratic presidential candidate George McGovern in 1972.

choose to have an abortion. In 1974, the Supreme Court affirmed this right under certain conditions.

Both the Equal Rights Amendment and the right of a woman to choose to have an abortion were controversial issues in the 1970s, and they are still controversial today. Yet some of Shirley's ideas which once seemed controversial no longer do. She argued for and won more money for early childhood education and successfully co-sponsored a bill which gave maids and domestics a minimum wage. During Shirley's third term in Congress, she served on a committee which accepted her recommendations to make it easier for new members of Congress to *choose* their committees, instead of having to accept whatever the Speaker of the House doles out. This was a major reform which helps new members of Congress. And she was chair of the special Congressional Black Caucus Task Force on Haitian Refugees. Its members recommended that the United States government permit Haitian refugees, who were running away from a terrible dictator, to stay in this country.

The longer Shirley Chisholm stayed in politics, the more she realized how important it was to make Americans think about the problems of women and minorities. In 1972, she decided to run for president of the United States. She believed that she could speak for both women and minorities better than anyone else who might run. Although she knew that she had very little chance of being nominated by the Democratic party, she campaigned in thirty-three states. "I can be an instrument for change," she told her audiences. She was disappointed that more women did not support her, but she was proud of her effort. She had shown that an African-American woman could be a serious candidate. That year, Richard Nixon, a Republican, won his second term as president. He ran against Democrat George McGovern.

After the presidential campaign, Shirley continued to serve in the House of Representatives for another ten years. In 1977, she and Conrad were divorced, and she married Arthur Hardwick, a politician.

When Shirley left Congress, she became a professor at Mt. Holyoke College in South Hadley, Massachusetts, where she taught courses in government for several years. When she retired from teaching, she and Arthur moved to a small town outside of Buffalo, New York.

Both men and women say Shirley Chisholm's most important accomplishment was to be a role model for women in America. Not only did she speak out for members of her race, but she spoke out for all women as well.

© Diana Mara Henry.

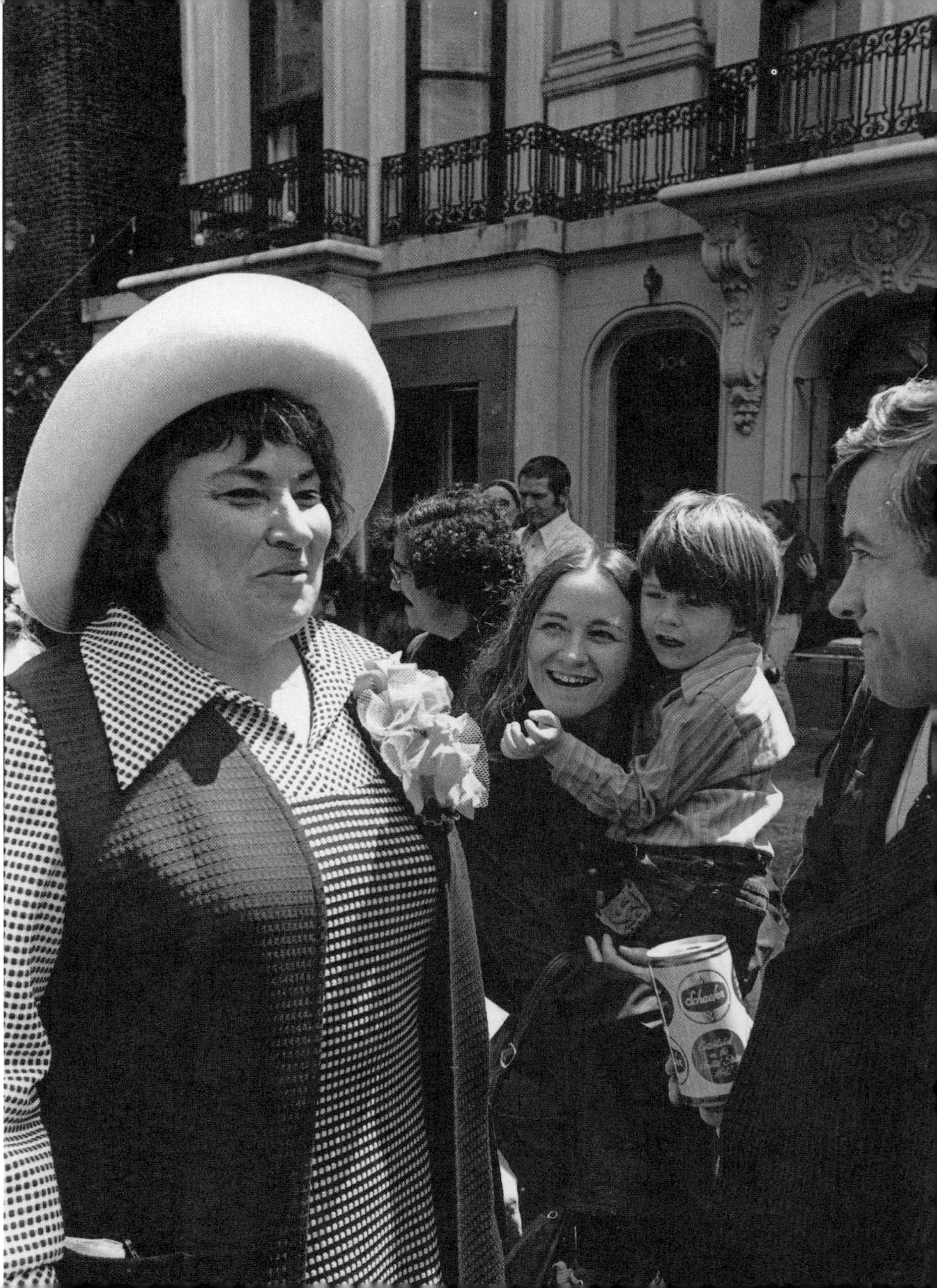

BELLA ABZUG
"Bring Congress Back to the People"

DEMOCRAT OF NEW YORK

United States Representative: January 1971–January 1977

"I always knew Bella would make it," said her mother, Esther Tanklefsky Savitzky, at her daughter's victory party in 1970. "She always did her homework and practiced without being told to."

No wonder Bella Abzug's mother was proud. Her daughter had just been elected to the House of Representatives from the Nineteenth Congressional District in New York City. She'd beaten a congressman whom Democrats in Greenwich Village (a section of the city famous for its artists, musicians, and writers) hadn't been able to oust in five tries.

If Mrs. Savitzky had faith in her daughter, Bella Abzug had faith in the people who had sent her to Congress. She knew the folks in her district wanted her to do the right thing. For Bella, the right thing was to be "a voice of change" for America's underprivileged and to stop the Vietnam War. This war had divided Americans. Some believed it was necessary to fight in Vietnam, a country in Southeast Asia, in order to stop the spread of communism there. Others, like Bella, believed the conflict was a civil war between two parts of Vietnam, the North and the South. They opposed America's involvement in the war and thought the Vietnamese people alone should decide how their country should be ruled. But all Americans wanted the war to end. Many of our soldiers had been killed or wounded there since 1965, when President Johnson first sent American troops to fight on the side of the South Vietnamese.

Bella campaigns for Congress in 1972.

"I always thought that the law was an instrument of change," Bella once said. But as a young lawyer in the 1950s, she had found that the law didn't always work in favor of women, minorities, and the poor. When she was elected to the House of Representatives in 1970, Bella was anxious to draft new laws to help these groups. But she believed that the first order of business was to end the war. The sooner it was over, the sooner Congress could use the money once spent for the war on programs to help people at home.

Bella Savitzky was born in the Bronx on July 24, 1920, the second daughter of Russian Jewish immigrants. Her father, Emanuel Savitzky, did many things to support his family. He was a butcher and also worked as a bookkeeper and sold insurance. Her mother, Esther, was a home-maker, but she also helped her husband whenever he needed her.

Bella's grandfather babysat for her and her older sister, Helene. "He was a very religious man," Bella said. "And I used to go to synagogue with him a lot."

Bella with her grandfather, Wolf Tanklefsky, in 1925.

As a child, Bella learned how to *daven* (to pray aloud with great feeling) and to read Hebrew. Her grandfather would brag to his cronies about his granddaughter's skill. But when little Bella got bigger, she was sent upstairs to the synagogue balcony because in Orthodox Judaism (a branch of Judaism which observes all of the ancient laws), men and women are not permitted to sit together during religious services. "Many people have suggested," said Bella, "that it was those early days up in the balcony that got me interested in women's rights."

School, Hebrew lessons, and friends didn't fill up all of Bella's time. She also wanted to learn to play the violin. Helene played the piano, so Bella asked her parents for music lessons, too. Her mother said no, because Helene had to be pushed to practice. "I had enough with your sister and the piano," she told her younger daughter.

That didn't stop independent Bella. She had a friend who was studying violin, and one day she waited on the steps of her friend's house for the violin teacher to come out. She brought him home and told her mother that this person would teach her to play the violin. Mrs. Savitzky relented, and Bella studied long and hard to learn her favorite instrument.

Bella's interest in politics began in fourth grade when she decided to run for class president. The principal thought that Bella was too outspoken and a troublemaker. He removed her name from the list of candidates. But Bella got her friends to vote for her anyway by writing her name on their ballots. And she won. "Although I didn't understand it at the time, it was a forecast of the future," she said. She was learning how to fight for what she believed in.

When she was eleven, Bella made her first speech—in a subway car. She and her friends were helping to collect money for the Jewish National Fund, an organization that helped Jewish settlers in Palestine (now Israel). Thousands of Jewish people had fled there to escape anti-Semitism in Europe. Bella sympathized. She herself had felt the painful sting of anti-Semitism as a child in the Bronx. She said she had "a dream that there would be this land that was free of discrimination against Jews. I lived in a lot of places in the Bronx where [Jews] were very much a minority."

Just before Bella entered high school, her father died. It was in the midst of the Great Depression, a time when millions of people were out of work. Although there was a little money from an insurance policy, Bella's mother had to find a way to support her family and send Helene to college. She went to work as a cashier and saleswoman in a department store. Bella helped, too. She took a job as a camp counselor in the summer. Once school started, she taught Hebrew and Jewish history and culture to children on weekends. And she continued her own Jewish studies at a special Hebrew high school after regular school. She missed her father greatly, and she knew how much he had wanted his children to continue their education.

"My mother was always supportive," said Bella. "She thought I could do anything. She used to meet me after school and take all my books so I could go to Hebrew school. She'd bring me my Hebrew books [in exchange]. If I got in trouble in school and was scolded by the teacher, I'd come home and tell my mother. She would go to school and scold the teacher!"

Bella didn't know any lawyers when she was growing up. Yet it seemed very natural to her to go to law school after she graduated from Hunter College in 1942. "I came from a home where there was a clear sense of social justice. And I really believed that if I could become a lawyer, I could set things straight," she said. Bella was accepted at Columbia University Law School in New York City. She was such an excellent student that at the end of her first year, she was chosen to be an editor of the *Columbia Law Review,* a journal which publishes important articles on law.

Bella was still in law school when she got married. She had met Martin Abzug on a bus in 1942 when both were going to the same concert. "My first reaction to Bella was wonderment," he told a reporter years later. "I never met anyone like her." Bella had boundless energy. She was determined to make the world a better place for all people. Before Bella and Martin married in 1944, they agreed that Bella would be a wife, a mother, *and* a lawyer. Martin, who was a novelist and then a stockbroker,

Bella and her family. From left to right: Martin, Bella, Eve, and Liz.

was proud of his ambitious wife. They had two daughters, "Eegee" (Eve Gail), born in 1949, and "Liz" (Isobel Jo), born in 1952.

Bella's first job was with a law firm which specialized in labor law. She defended workers who believed their employers had broken laws which were supposed to protect them. When Bella was not defending clients in the courtroom, she organized people to work for their rights. Once she led a tenants' strike because a landlord had not made proper repairs on his building. Since the tenants had no heat or hot water, they refused to pay their rent. The landlord was embarrassed when the newspapers reported the story, and he made the repairs. Bella had a knack for inspiring people to work to change things they believed were wrong. Besides being a lawyer, she was also a social activist. In 1947, she opened her own office.

From the 1940s to the 1960s, Bella devoted herself to three major causes. The first was civil rights. As a lawyer, she defended those she thought were being unfairly treated because of their race. One case, which she eventually lost, made a lasting impression on her. As a lawyer for the American Civil Liberties Union, she was chosen to handle the appeal of Willie McGee, a black man in Mississippi. He had been convicted of raping a white woman and sentenced to death. In the 1950s, it was against the law in many states for whites and blacks to date each other. And this man had dated a white woman. When their romance was discovered, the woman said he had raped her. In the South, an African-American found guilty of raping a white woman could get the death penalty. Bella appealed the case all the way to the Supreme Court, but in the end her client was executed. This injustice made Bella more determined than ever to work to change unfair laws.

Her second cause was to stop the lies Senator Joseph McCarthy of Wisconsin was spreading about many American citizens. Bella defended artists and writers who were fired from their jobs or even faced jail when Senator McCarthy accused them of being Communists. It took several years before Mr. McCarthy was censured by his colleagues in the Senate. Senator Margaret Chase Smith was the first senator to warn the country that McCarthy was a fraud.

Her third cause was to put an end to nuclear testing and the competition between the U.S. and Soviet Union to build nuclear bombs. In 1961, after it was discovered that fallout (radioactive material that falls on the earth after a nuclear bomb explosion) from testing the bombs put a dangerous, cancer-causing chemical in our milk supply, Bella and her women friends started a group called Women Strike for Peace (WSP). This group gained supporters from all over the country. That year, the women marched in front of the White House and at the United Nations to protest the testing of nuclear weapons. In New York City, WSP worked to elect members of Congress who agreed with their cause.

Thousands of people around the world joined the protest against nuclear bombs. In 1963, President John F. Kennedy and leaders in the Soviet Union and Great Britain signed an agreement to stop testing nuclear weapons in the air, on the ground, and in the sea. This was an important first step in limiting nuclear testing.

By 1970, Bella had other concerns, too. There seemed to be no end in sight to the conflict in Vietnam. To help bring the war to an end, Bella decided to run for Congress herself instead of supporting other candidates. She wanted to unseat her representative, Democrat Leonard Farbstein, because he didn't share her desire to bring a swift end to the Vietnam War or to limit nuclear weapons. Many Democrats in her district agreed with Bella. One Democratic club had been trying to oust Congressman Farbstein for years. But Mr. Farbstein always won in both the primary and the general elections.

Bella thought she could beat Mr. Farbstein. She knew her friends in WSP would support her campaign. But she had to get the approval of the Village Independent Democrats, the Democratic club in Greenwich Village, where she lived. The club's leaders were the ones who selected the people to run for office. When she paid these men a visit, she announced, "I'm your candidate."

"You're kidding," the men replied.

"No, I'm not kidding."

"But you're the one who always *helps* us with the elections. You're our ally."

"My people have their own candidate this time," she answered. "And I'm it."

The leaders of the club were not convinced. They had at least four men who wanted to run for Congress. But finally Bella got them to support her. Now she had to win the election.

Bella didn't have money for flashy television ads. From early morning until midnight, she went out on the streets to campaign. Her slogan was "This Woman Belongs in the House." She always wore one of her colorful, floppy hats. (Her hats became her trademark.) "I used to stand on the sidewalks near the big housing projects with a microphone and speak up to the windows," Bella said. "People would open their windows and listen to me, and that's how I won the election!"

Of course, there were hundreds of women from Women Strike for Peace campaigning, too. And members of the Village Independent Democrats rallied to her support as well. They knocked on doors, handed out campaign literature, and staffed her campaign headquarters. Not only did Bella Abzug defeat Mr. Farbstein in the primary election, but in November she won a landslide victory against the Republican candidate.

On January 3, 1971, Bella Abzug was sworn in as the congresswoman from New York's Nineteenth Congressional District. She was one of just eleven women in the House of Representatives. So many of her supporters came to see her sworn in that they overflowed her office. After the official ceremony, Bella went to the steps of the Capitol, where Brooklyn congresswoman Shirley Chisholm swore her in again in front of her well wishers. Bella promised to work to end the war in Vietnam and redirect the nation's resources towards peaceful purposes. On her first day in Congress, she introduced a resolution calling for all troops to be withdrawn from Southeast Asia by July fourth.

When Bella opened her congressional office in New York City, she hired a social worker and a community organizer. She wanted a staff who could help constituents with their problems. One man who had recently opened a pizza parlor came to the office. He said that the electric company was overcharging him and wouldn't stop. Bella's aide got him his refund—fifteen hundred dollars! It was enough for him to expand his business.

Congresswoman Abzug worked eighteen hours a day, seven days a week. She would introduce bills, make speeches on the floor of the House, talk to reporters, fly around the country to speak to college students and women's groups, and meet with constituents at home in New York City or in her Washington, D.C., office. When she was in Washington, Bella was often so busy she only had time to eat fast food. She gained more than forty pounds, but she said it was "voters before calories!"

Her day often began at six AM, when she and Congresswoman Edith Greene swam in the House of Representatives's pool. This was the only time the women could swim, for the men, who had the pool from nine in the morning until nine at night, swam nude. One morning Bella said to the lifeguard, "I guess this pool is really jumping later on."

"No," he replied, "very few people ever swim here."

That was all feisty Bella had to hear! She went to the head of the gym committee and said, "Tell the boys to put their suits on. We're coming in!" And that's how Bella Abzug made it possible for women members of the House to use the pool whenever they wanted. It was one small victory for women.

Other victories were not so fast in coming. As one of four hundred thirty-five representatives, with many different goals, Bella often could not get things done her way. A bill which she and Shirley Chisholm co-sponsored to fund affordable child care twenty-four hours a day passed in both the House and Senate but was vetoed by the president. And her efforts to bring the Vietnam War to an end were not successful. The best Congress was willing to do in 1971 was to vote for the Vietnam Disengagement Act, which called for the end of the war within two years. Bella tried to persuade her colleagues to vote to end the military draft, but that effort failed. The war did not end until 1975.

When Bella asked to serve on the Armed Services Committee, she was turned down. Not since Congresswoman Margaret Chase Smith served in the House had a woman won assignment to that committee. Instead, Bella was put on the Government Operations Committee. During her first term, she pushed through the Freedom of Information Act, which had been languishing in the committee since 1954. This important bill, which was signed into law in 1975, gives citizens the right to see any files the United States government has been keeping on their activities. It also allows writers and historians to examine papers from different branches of the government.

Bella also served on the Committee on Public Works, which approves contracts for repairing highways, railroads, and bridges. For many years, women and minorities who owned businesses had complained that they didn't get the chance to work on these projects. Bella sponsored a bill that made it easier for such businesses to have the chance to compete for work. The bill became law. Bella Abzug and Shirley Chisholm introduced a bill to force factory owners to clean up the lakes and rivers their manufacturing had polluted. That bill also became law.

But perhaps the most satisfying moment for Bella came on October 12, 1971. On that day, after months of exciting debate, the House of Representatives voted to approve the Equal Rights Amendment. The Senate approved the ERA in 1972. An amendment to the Constitution, however, must be approved by thirty-eight state legislatures. Only thirty-five states ratified the Equal Rights Amendment, so it did not pass. Many opponents of the ERA were afraid that if there was a war and men were drafted, women would have to fight, too.

Bella was a congresswoman who didn't mind shaking things up. She was always direct in asking questions, and she spoke out in plain English when she thought people were not truthful. Many of her colleagues respected her, even those with whom she disagreed. Congresswoman Millicent Fenwick, who often voted differently from her Democratic colleague, admired Bella for her courage in speaking her mind. "Bella always represented the people who elected her," Millicent said. In turn, Bella admired Millicent's honesty and open-mindedness on difficult issues.

Bella Abzug served for six years in the House of Representatives. In 1976, she decided to run for the Senate. In a hard-fought battle against

Bella speaks at a party held while she was running for the Senate in 1976.

Daniel Patrick Moynihan, she lost by less than one percent of the vote. Bella was angry and disappointed. But when she had some time to reflect on the loss, she said, "I fight hard, and I try to win. If I don't win, I keep fighting." In fact, her tough style won her the nickname of "Bellicose Bella," and in 1977 a hurricane was named for her!

Bella Abzug continues to fight for what she believes in. Today, with other women all around the world, she works to save the environment. She often travels to Eastern Europe to teach women who had once lived under communism learn to become leaders in their new democracies. And she still practices law from her Greenwich Village office.

Bella has never lost her faith in the ability of the people to change the world. "I think there are going to be enormous changes in America," she said in 1991. "People ended the war in Vietnam. It was the people who wanted to impeach President Nixon, and it was the people who finally had enough of Senator Joe McCarthy. I believe that people, given the truth and the freedom to organize, will act in their own best interests."

BARBARA JORDAN
"I Always Wanted to Be Something Unusual"

DEMOCRAT OF TEXAS

United States Representative: January 1973–January 1979

In 1936, the year in which Barbara Charline Jordan was born, her home state of Texas was racially segregated. There were segregated schools, restaurants, taxis, lunch counters, hospital wards, swimming pools, and churches. A black police officer could not arrest a white person. Black people had to drink from separate public water fountains, and they had to use separate toilets when they shopped in department stores.

The city of Houston, Texas, is divided into different sections, or wards. The Fifth Ward of Houston, where Barbara grew up, had many unpaved streets and hardly any streetlights. Her parents owned a narrow, two-bedroom house called a "shotgun shack." It got that strange name because someone once said that if you shot a gun through the front door, the bullet would go straight through and out the back door.

The Jordan house on Campbell Street sheltered a family of seven: Barbara's parents, Benjamin and Arlyne Jordan, her Grandmother and Grandfather Jordan, and the three Jordan sisters, Rose Mary, Bennie, and Barbara. The two bedrooms were for Barbara's parents and grandparents. At first, she and her sisters slept on a foldout bed in the dining room. As the youngest, Barbara got stuck sleeping in the middle! Later, her father added a bedroom for the girls.

Grandfather Jordan was a Baptist minister, and Barbara's home was deeply religious. When she was eleven, her father became a minister as well, and at twelve, Barbara asked to be baptized in her grandfather's church.

Barbara Jordan in 1990.

As a child, Barbara often felt her life was full of "no's" and "don'ts": no dancing, no movies, don't go into other people's houses. Barbara and her dad argued a lot over these "no's" and "don'ts." But when she became an adult, she understood that her father "brought a stability to my growing-up years even though he was very stern."

Life for Barbara and her sisters centered on their home, church, and school. She never dreamed she could live a life different from her mother's—washing (by hand, for there was no washing machine), ironing, cooking, and cleaning for the family. It was the life that Barbara and her girlfriends believed was in store for them. "I didn't know I had a choice," she said. Yet she knew, "I always wanted to be something unusual."

There was one person who always knew Barbara was special. That man was Grandfather Patten, her mother's father. He was her ally, someone who never said no but was also very wise.

Grandfather Patten lived in the Fourth Ward, a section of Houston even poorer than Barbara's neighborhood. His rented house did not have electricity or indoor plumbing. Every Sunday after church, however, the whole Jordan family would join Grandmother and Grandfather Patten for dinner at their house.

After dinner, when her sisters went home to learn their Bible verses, Barbara was allowed to stay with her grandfather. He was in the junk business and had a large wagon with two mules. He paid Barbara to help him sort out the things he had collected over the week. He would tell his favorite granddaughter not to be afraid to be different from other children. "You just trot your own horse and don't get into the same rut as everyone else," Grandfather Patten said. He would also scrounge up treasures just for her. At one time, she had three bicycles!

When she was ten, Barbara wanted a motor scooter. "I told my grandfather I needed to get around fast. He said that was a very good idea, and he would get me this motor scooter. But since I would be moving along the streets of Houston, he needed to go to my mother and see if she would agree for me to own a motor scooter."

Barbara
at about
age ten.

Courtesy of Barbara Jordan.

Not surprisingly, Barbara's mother said no. So Grandfather Patten said, "I would get you the motor scooter, but your mother has the best argument. Your dress cannot be flying up all the time around Houston."

"And so, I never got it," she said.

Barbara attended Phillis Wheatley High School, which was named for a famous black poet. Because the school was segregated, all her teachers and fellow students were black. Barbara found several teachers who "knew what it would take for me to be successful in life." Unfortunately, there were other teachers who were what Barbara called "color-struck."

"Color-struck" people believed, Barbara said, that "if they could just lighten their black skin, they were going to do better." And sometimes such teachers ignored the darker-skinned students, such as Barbara, and favored those with lighter skin.

But Barbara knew that what mattered most "had to be what was in my head, not the color of the skin that was covering my head. Nothing could make me say I wanted to go out and get that Black and White Bleach Cream."

In high school, Barbara excelled in debating. She learned to think on her feet, and her beautiful, resonant voice always attracted attention. She was so good that the first time she entered an oratorical contest, in Waco, Texas, she won the first prize of fifty dollars. Debating taught her, Barbara said, "the power of words."

In 1952, Barbara followed in her sister Bennie's footsteps and enrolled in Texas Southern University (TSU) in Houston. Like Barbara's high school, Texas Southern had only black teachers and students. She joined the TSU Debating and Oratorical Society, where she found "a window on the world which I would not otherwise have experienced."

In the 1950s, many black organizations, and some white ones, began to challenge the laws which maintained segregation. Individuals were causing changes, too. Barbara's debating coach, Dr. Thomas Freeman, was a black minister who had graduated from the University of Chicago. Because he had studied at a university which was integrated (open to all students regardless of color), he made sure that TSU students had opportunities to debate at white universities in the South and at integrated universities in the North. This experience made Barbara see new possibilities and also brought her into some uncomfortable situations.

The debate team traveled all over the country in Dr. Freeman's yellow Mercury. Otis King, Barbara's debating partner for all four years at TSU, recalled one trip in 1953 from Houston to Florida. "Now that was during the time of segregation in the South, and there was a lot of difficulty finding places to eat and to sleep. Dr. Freeman always would fry chicken before we left, and mostly we'd eat it before we left his church parking lot while he was taking care of last-minute business."

But hunger would strike the travelers while they were on the road. Then there was a problem. Some restaurants simply refused to serve African-Americans, and others had a front entrance for white people and a back one for black people. Often blacks were not permitted to use the bathrooms at all. Barbara recalled, "Dr. Freeman used to say to us, 'I'm not going to take you in through the back door at any of these places. I will go to the back door, get the food, and bring it out to you so we can eat in the car.' "

Sometimes the team members had to drive through the night because no motels would accept them. At other times, however, Dr. Freeman had friends along the way who would put up the students in their homes or in the local churches.

Dr. Freeman was proud of his team. In 1954, it integrated a debate at the all-white Baylor University in Houston. "That was the first time they let blacks into the tournament," Dr. Freeman said. "Barbara won first place in oratory." The students went on to debate the University of Chicago team, a particularly fearsome one. They wanted to beat Chicago because it was Dr. Freeman's school. When they trounced Chicago's debate team, Barbara and her teammates were thrilled.

But Barbara never forgot that first trip to Chicago for another reason. "I felt as if I had left the old country and moved into some new dynamic scene. We could go in the front door of hotels and go in the front door of these restaurants and sit down and have a meal. It gave us an appreciation for what integration would mean for us if it ever came South."

In that same year, 1954, the United States Supreme Court opened the door to integration throughout the country when it ruled that separate schools for black students were not equal to those provided for white students. A year later, a black woman named Rosa Parks broke a city law in Montgomery, Alabama. The law ordered African-Americans to sit in the back or middle seats of a bus, and to give up the seats in the middle if a white person wanted them. Many other states in the South had this law, too. When Rosa Parks refused to give up her seat in the middle of the bus, she was arrested. This so angered the black citizens of Montgomery that for more than a year, they refused to ride the city buses. This kind of group action is called a "boycott." It was organized by a young black minister named Martin Luther King, Jr.

In 1956, the Supreme Court ruled that laws such as those requiring black citizens to sit in the backs of buses were unconstitutional. At last a person of color had the same right as a white person to sit anywhere in a bus. Now, not only would segregated schools and segregated seating in buses no longer be allowed, but segregated drinking fountains, public bathrooms, and restaurants would be against the law as well.

Barbara was elated. Although she knew there would be a lot of resistance from those white people in the South who wanted to keep things the way they were, she had seen that unjust laws could be changed.

When she graduated from Texas Southern University in 1956, Barbara was determined to study law at an integrated university. She chose Boston University. Her father agreed to pay her way. He said, "This is more money than I have ever spent on anything or anyone. But if you want to go, we'll manage."

Barbara knew there was no money for her to come home for holidays. "Once you get there, you're there," her father told her. Barbara spent a lonely time in the dormitory that first Christmas, but she never complained.

The classes at law school were harder than any Barbara had ever taken. During her first year, she never got more than three or four hours of sleep a night. "I didn't look around for excuses for nonachievement. I just decided what I had to do, and I did it. That doesn't work for everybody, but it worked for me." She wrote in her autobiography that she felt she was doing sixteen years of remedial work in thinking.

Barbara graduated from law school in 1959 and returned to Houston. She had no money to open a law office, so she began her law practice at her mother's dining room table. Within three years, her practice grew enough for her to open a real office. Soon she became involved in Fifth Ward politics, too.

In 1960, Barbara campaigned for the election of President John Kennedy and Vice-President Lyndon Johnson. The local Democrats recognized her superb organizational and speaking abilities. Some thought she should run for the Texas House of Representatives. Barbara agreed to be the candidate from the Fifth Ward in 1962 and again in 1964. She lost both times but was not discouraged. She was gaining experience in meeting voters and listening to their problems. In 1966, Barbara ran for the Texas State Senate and won.

There are just thirty-one senators in the Texas legislature, and there hadn't been a black senator since 1883! Barbara Jordan became the first black woman ever to serve as a Texas state senator. She was only thirty-one years old.

Barbara was determined to know more about the rules of the legislature than the men who had been there for years. Before she was sworn in,

Photo by Yoichi Okamoto. Courtesy of the Lyndon Baines Johnson Library, Austin, Texas.

she learned all of the written and unwritten rules that told how a senator should act. "I had a tremendous amount of faith in my own capacity," Barbara told a reporter on the *Texas Observer*. "I know how to read and write and think, so I have no fear."

At the end of her first year, Barbara won the Outstanding Senator Award, given by her colleagues. During her years in the Texas Senate, she worked to pass a law which would raise the pay that farmworkers received. This law was very important to both Mexican-Americans and African-Americans, since many of them were farmworkers. She also learned that stopping a bad bill from becoming a law was sometimes as important as getting a good bill passed. In her first term, she worked to defeat a sales tax on food and drugs, for she knew such a tax would hurt poorer people the most.

In 1967, Barbara received a telegram from President Lyndon Johnson (who was a Texan himself, and who had been watching Barbara's career in the state Senate). He asked her to come to a meeting at the White House. "Well, I guess I will go," Barbara said. But she really thought, "Lyndon Johnson probably doesn't know who I am, and my name probably just slipped in somehow."

At the White House, Barbara was seated at a long table with black and white civil rights leaders from all over the country. President Johnson was

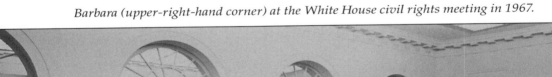

Barbara (upper-right-hand corner) at the White House civil rights meeting in 1967.

Barbara with President Johnson, about 1966.

determined to pass the most far-reaching civil rights laws ever proposed in America. One law would be a fair housing act which would make it a crime to deny a person the right to rent or buy a house or apartment because of the color of his or her skin.

At one point, President Johnson interrupted the discussion and said, "Barbara, what do you think?" The president of the United States had called her by name!

Later, while Barbara was still a Texas state senator, the president asked her to serve on a special commission to see that all Americans received a minimum income. "What we were doing," said Barbara, "was laying the groundwork for a minimum income guarantee for poor people." This idea was never acted upon by Congress.

Barbara served in the Texas Senate until 1972. Then she decided to run for the House of Representatives of the United States Congress. Since she was the best-known African-American woman in all of Texas, she did not face a difficult campaign. Barbara became the first black woman ever elected to Congress from the South.

When she won, Lyndon Johnson immediately called to congratulate her. Even though he was no longer president (Richard Nixon was), Barbara asked him which committee assignments she should request.

She wanted to be on the Armed Services Committee and the Government Operations Committee, or possibly on the Judiciary Committee. Mr. Johnson strongly recommended the Judiciary Committee, and that is the assignment she got.

Soon after Barbara was sworn in as a member of the House in January 1973, very disturbing news began to surface concerning the way President Nixon had conducted his reelection campaign in 1972. It turned out that the president had agreed to let his staff find someone to break into the Democratic national headquarters to steal important documents. When the break-in, at a building called the Watergate, was discovered, the president denied knowing about it. But as the evidence mounted, it became clear that President Nixon had lied and then tried to cover up what had happened. It was the job of the Judiciary Committee to decide if the president had broken the law.

Early in July 1974, after months of investigation by federal authorities, the House Judiciary Committee met to see if there was enough evidence to call for President Nixon's impeachment. Impeachment is a charge of grave misconduct brought against a federal official. If the House of Representatives finds that there is enough evidence, then the accused person is tried by members of the Senate. This was only the second time in the history of our country that Congress had considered impeaching a president.

On July 25, the members of the Judiciary Committee went on national television to tell the people of the United States what they were going to recommend.

When it was Barbara's turn to speak, she reminded Americans that when the Constitution was written in 1787, blacks were not counted as part of "We, the people." Most of them were slaves. She spoke in careful, measured tones. Her rich, powerful voice, tinged with a soft Texas accent, was spellbinding. She explained how solemn this occasion was to her, and how much faith she had in the Constitution. "I felt somehow for many years that George Washington and Alexander Hamilton just left me out by mistake," she said. "But, through the process of amendment, interpretation, and court decision, I have finally been included in 'We, the people.'" She said that no individual, including the president of the United States, could be permitted to destroy the Constitution by lying to the Congress and the American people in order to win an election. Her review of the evidence against President Nixon led her to vote for impeachment. So did the majority of the committee.

Before the full House of Representatives could debate the committee's recommendations, Mr. Nixon resigned. He was the first president in our history to do so. Vice-President Gerald Ford then became president.

With the Watergate scandal over, Barbara could turn all her attention to legislation. Her goal in Congress was to be "a good member and to serve the people of my district." She said, however, "I did not see myself as representing specifically the interests of black people. I knew that whatever I did was representative of the interests of black people."

Among her proudest accomplishments was to expand the Voting Rights Act, passed in 1965 to make certain no American citizens lost their right to vote because they were poor or did not speak English. Until 1964, many southern states made people pay money if they wanted to vote. This fee was called a "poll tax" and was aimed at keeping African-Americans from voting. The Twenty-fourth Amendment to the Constitution, ratified in 1964, says a poll tax is illegal. Even so, many states still tried to make black citizens pay money to vote. With the passage of the Voting Rights Act of 1965, the United States government could send officials to supervise elections and ensure that no poll tax was charged. But it turned out that other minorities, such as Native Americans, Asian-Americans, and Latinos, were often not allowed to vote because they couldn't read or write English. In 1973, Barbara sponsored legislation to give these Americans their voting rights, too. Always concerned that ordinary people be treated fairly, Barbara also sponsored the Consumer Goods Pricing Act of 1975. This law makes sure that many items people purchase are fairly priced.

In 1976, Barbara Jordan became the first woman, as well as the first African-American, to give a major speech at a Democratic National

Convention. As she told Americans of her strong faith in the United States government, her stirring words made many people think she deserved to be the Democratic choice for vice-president. But Barbara was content to serve for another term in the House of Representatives.

Barbara Jordan decided not to run for reelection in 1978. Now she was ready to become a professor at the Lyndon B. Johnson School of Public Affairs at the University of Texas in Austin. Also, she had discovered that she had multiple sclerosis (a disease that would eventually force her to use a wheelchair). But Barbara didn't tell people about her illness then, and many were shocked when she chose the quieter life of a college professor.

Barbara's teaching career has been very rewarding. She teaches a course on ethics in politics, that is, on the proper behavior for people who serve in our government. Her goal is to "leave a 'scratch,' let us say, on the next generation. If I can get through to my students what it is like to be a public servant, then I will have my legacy carried on by others."

But Barbara Jordan remains involved in politics, as much as her health allows. In 1992 she was again chosen to speak at the Democratic National Convention. She believes that for government to run well, good, honest individuals have to serve the people. "Politics," said Barbara Jordan, "is an honorable profession." And a good politician is one who "acts in the public interest, who is truthful, credible, honest, and who is able to turn from greed and selfhood and think in terms of others."

Barbara teaches a class at the University of Texas in 1983.

PATRICIA SCHROEDER
Standing Up for the American Family

DEMOCRAT OF COLORADO

United States Representative: January 1973–Present

Pat Schroeder moved so many times when she was little that she developed a surefire way to make friends quickly: "Just put your toys out on the block and see who shows up," she said, breaking into one of her famous toothy grins. Then, in a more serious voice, she added, "It's never easy to make friends as the new kid in town. And kids who move early in the summer don't have any way to make connections. You have to do whatever you can." Her father once said that growing up was really difficult for his daughter, who "was always the new girl in town, who wore glasses, and was always too tall for her age."

Pat's dad was reared on a farm in Nebraska. He started out in construction, then went into aviation, and finally began his own aviation insurance company. His work required many moves, and by the time Pat started high school, she had lived in six different towns in four states.

Patricia Nell Scott was born in Portland, Oregon, on July 30, 1940. She attended grade school in Texas, junior high school in Ohio, and high school in Iowa. She graduated from the University of Minnesota in 1961 and from Harvard Law School in Massachusetts in 1964.

Living—and flying—all around the country didn't seem odd to Pat. Her dad, Lee Scott, was a licensed pilot. For as long as she could remember, "We always had an airplane." Pat learned to fly when she was a teenager. Her younger brother, Mike, and her mother, Bernice, a first grade teacher, learned to fly, too.

Patricia Schroeder at about age six.

A fellow student, Jim Schroeder, took note of Pat's love of flying when he met her at Harvard Law School in 1961. Jim had been a pilot in the United States Navy. "We hit it off pretty well," Jim recalled. So well, in fact, that they were married a year later. After graduation from law school, the young couple headed west to Denver, Colorado, where both Pat and Jim practiced law and Pat taught law courses at two colleges as well.

In 1966 their son, Scott, was born. A daughter, Jamie, was born in 1970. Pat Schroeder managed the difficult job of juggling marriage, mother-hood, and a demanding career. There were three good reasons why Pat was able to do this. One was her sense of humor. She could always laugh at herself. "I try to take whatever I'm doing seriously, but I've never taken myself very seriously," she said. The second was that Jim Schroeder willingly shared the responsibilities of home and children.

The third reason was Pat's efficient work habits. From the time she was a child, Pat had always worked at top speed. Even in grade school, she knew how to organize her time. Because Pat was a quick learner, teachers tried to keep her busy. "When I think about it, in grade school I had a zillion jobs. I tutored first graders and I did this and that. But I never thought of it as being different. I thought that I had to get done with my work because I had all these jobs!"

Perhaps teachers gave Pat a lot of responsibility because she looked mature for her age. "I think I was the height I am now when I was about eleven years old," she said. (She is five feet, seven inches tall.) Pat believes that taller children tend to be treated as if they are older.

Still, being tall definitely had its down side. "All the boys came to about my waist. And every time I went to get on a bus and I wanted to pay the child's fare, the bus driver would say, 'No way!'" Her brother Mike once joked, "In junior high school, she looked like a twig with glasses . . . skin and bones, tall and gangly."

Pat and Mike learned how to handle money when they were quite young. Starting at age nine, Pat was given an allowance at the beginning of each month. "It was enough to cover school lunches, clothing—everything. And if I blew it the first day, then somehow I had to figure out how to get to the end of the month," Pat said. She remembers putting money aside for months to buy a winter coat. Budgeting was a big responsibility, and one that was a source of many serious family discussions.

Most kids in grade and middle school, Pat observed, never have to think about money. They never have to plan. "My parents tried to turn us into self-starters, and it worked for me because I knew that they wouldn't bail me out." When Pat and Jim's children reached fifth grade, they, too, were entrusted with monthly allowances for all of their needs.

Pat has always fought for what she believes is right. When she was a teenager, she joined a group of students and adults who supported the right of supermarkets to carry a brand of bread called Profile. Some people believed that little children shouldn't be allowed to see the picture on the bread wrapper. (It was a silhouette of a shapely woman!) They demanded that the bread be removed from the shelves. Pat believed then, and still believes now, that people who try to censor (control) what other people see or read or buy are wrong. The group that Pat belonged to wrote letters to the newspapers and carried picket signs at the supermarket urging the store not to give in to those who would deny people their choice of bread. Eventually, Pat's group won its case.

Pat's activism continued after her marriage. Soon after she and Jim moved to Denver, both became leaders in their community in protesting the Vietnam War.

The Schroeders were both Democrats. Jim was active in the First District Democratic club and served on the committee which selected candidates to run for Congress. He came home from a meeting one evening in 1972 and told Pat she was the committee's choice to run for the House of Representatives. At first they both laughed, for they didn't think Pat could actually win the election. The well-liked Republican candidate who was running for reelection was supposed to be unbeatable. And Pat had never run for any political office before. But after thinking it over, she decided to give it her best shot. She had been speaking out against the Vietnam War for a long time. As a member of Congress, perhaps she could join colleagues who were opposed to the war and help bring it to an end.

Pat was interested in other issues, too. She wanted to help pass laws to give all children the opportunity for a good education. She understood the need for health care for all Americans and the need of elderly people to live in dignity. As the campaign progressed, more and more people listened to this earnest and well-informed young woman.

To the surprise of many, including the candidate herself, Patricia Scott Schroeder won the congressional election with 52 percent of the vote. Her victory was even more astonishing because President Richard Nixon, a Republican, won his second term that year in a landslide victory. He won in all but two states! Many Republican candidates for Congress were swept into office because voters who pulled down the lever for president then continued to pull the levers on the Republican line for the congressional candidates as well.

When thirty-two-year-old Democrat Pat Schroeder went off to Washington, Jim, two-year-old Jamie, and six-year-old Scott went, too. Pat held Jamie in her arms at her swearing-in ceremony. She liked to joke that she was the only member of Congress ever sworn in with a batch of diapers in her purse!

The first few months in Washington were especially hectic for the Schroeders. Jim had given up his law practice in Denver so that the whole family could move together. (Many members of Congress keep a small apartment in Washington while their families stay back in their home towns.) Pat and Jim agreed it was important to keep the family together. They found a house just outside the capital in nearby Virginia. Jim stayed at home until a housekeeper was hired and Scott was settled into school.

"It was a difficult adjustment," said Pat. She received no encouragement from other members of the House of Representatives. "I remember [Congresswoman] Bella Abzug, whom I'd never met, calling me when I got elected. 'I want to congratulate you on your election,' Bella said. 'But I understand you have small children, and you won't be able to do this.' And I thought, 'Well, if Bella doesn't think I can do this, then who does?' "

People even wrote Pat letters criticizing her for being in Congress. They said she "should stay home and take care of the children." Jim wholeheartedly supported Pat's career, but otherwise she felt very alone. "Nobody else was trying to do what I was doing," she said. At that time there were only thirteen women in Congress. None had very young children. Congressmen with families traditionally had wives to stay at home and care for the children. (It wasn't until 1984 that a day care center was established for the children of members of Congress and their staffs.) But with Jim's rock-solid help and Pat's determination, the Schroeder family settled in.

Soon Jim resumed his law career. Like Pat, he has a marvelous sense of humor. Jim was the founder of the "Denis Thatcher Society," for "men married to powerful women." Their motto is "Yes, dear," Jim jokes. (Denis Thatcher is the husband of the former prime minister of England, Margaret Thatcher.) But Jim is Pat's most trusted adviser.

Work is very important to Pat. And so is her family. Although she often takes a full briefcase home at night, she said, "I always tried to get out of my office fairly early, especially when the children were young. My goal was to have dinner with the family at least three times a week. It wasn't the kind of life where I gave the children rides everywhere, but I don't think that made me a worse mother." Yet even with a very heavy schedule and complicated life, Pat was with her children during important events. As a result, the Schroeder children sometimes had unusual birthday parties. One was held in the dining room for members of the House of Representatives! Later, when Scott played on his high school football team, she became a regular "football mom," attending almost all of his games and even washing and drying his practice uniform every night.

As the children grew older, they accompanied their mother on her trips back to Denver when she met with constituents. They traveled with Pat to the refugee camps in Thailand, where thousands of people had fled to escape violence in neighboring countries. (Pat was one of several members of Congress who went to study the situation in Thailand in order to recommend to the president what help the U.S. should provide.) Jamie and Scott also attended congressional meetings with their mother and learned how our lawmakers balance out different ideas in order to

Pat chairs a subcommittee of the House Armed Services Committee, about 1988.

pass fair laws. Pat's children have had the opportunity to see firsthand exactly what a member of Congress does in committee meetings. Afterwards they could discuss their opinions not only with their mother, but with other members of Congress. "And they had a good time," Pat said.

When Pat first went to Congress in 1973, she stuck to her campaign promise to work to end the war in Vietnam. She voted against sending more military aid to that country. (It would be another two years before the war ended.)

This did not mean she did not want our country to be strong. She wanted our country to have the best military in the world, but she also wanted to cut wasteful spending. She requested and was assigned a seat on the Armed Services Committee, becoming the first Democratic woman to serve there. As chairperson of the committee's Subcommittee on Research and Development, Pat made sure that special projects were needed and did not spend money unnecessarily. She is the leading advocate of defense burden-sharing, which calls upon our allies to share the cost of their military protection by the U.S. In 1993, Pat became the chairperson of the Subcommittee on Science and Technology of the Armed Services Committee. Now she and her committee will find ways to convert the research which created new and better weapons into technology that helps solve our peacetime problems.

Denver voters liked the way Pat did things, and she has continued to represent them. She hasn't ever had a serious challenge to her House seat. During her 1988 campaign, she won 70 percent of the votes. This was a year in which Republican George Bush won the presidential election in forty of the fifty states against the Democratic challenger, Michael Dukakis. Pat won resounding victories again in 1990 and 1992.

Congresswoman Pat Schroeder has a deep concern for military families. As part of her work on the Armed Services Committee, she has traveled all over the world, wherever our military men and women and their families are stationed, to learn what kinds of problems they face. She understands how difficult life can be for the wives and children of servicemen, for military families move on the average of every three years. It is hard for military wives to take jobs off the base because they never know how long they will live in one place. When husbands are sent on war missions, their families are left at home, often with little knowledge of where the men are stationed. In the past, if their husbands divorced them, military wives were left without any medical or other benefits, even if they had been married for twenty or thirty years. Pat Schroeder didn't think it was fair for military wives to be left unprotected. The careers of men in the military often depend upon the support of their wives.

In 1982, Congresswoman Schroeder sponsored legislation on behalf of divorced military wives. It passed into law. Now, divorced military wives can retain their health insurance and are entitled to share some of their former husbands' benefits.

Next, Pat worked to get the same benefits for former wives of men in the Central Intelligence Agency and the diplomatic service. These women faced special problems. Often their husbands were judged on their wives' ability to entertain properly, keep secrets, and even face grave danger. Congress finally agreed that if divorced, these women were entitled to retirement and survivor benefits.

In 1985, Pat introduced the Family Military Act, which sets standards for the care of children of men and women in the armed services during war. This law was tested during the Persian Gulf War in 1992 (Desert Storm), when military men and women were shipped overseas. In some cases, both parents were sent to the Persian Gulf, but thanks to this law, their children were quickly taken to the relatives designated by their parents. For children who stayed behind with the nonmilitary parent, special classes were held to help them cope with the fear of having a mother or father sent to a war zone. Before this, there were no provisions for caring for children whose parents were called to war.

The jewel in the crown of Pat Schroeder's career as a member of the House is her support of the American family. She is a member of the House Select Committee on Children, Youth, and Families. Pat knows that today's family does not always consist of a mother who stays at home with the children while the father goes out to work. In many two-parent families, both parents work, and the children need day care and after-school care. She knows that some families are "blended" families, with stepparents and stepchildren. Other families are headed by a single parent, most often a mother or grandmother. And she knows that in many families, there are elderly grandparents who must be cared for somehow, even though the young parents must work.

Pat Schroeder has made the problems of the modern American family a national issue. Her work to help families has brought her nationwide attention. She strongly supported the passage of the "Deadbeat Dads' Act," sponsored by Congresswoman Barbara Kennelly of Connecticut. This law makes it possible for single mothers to get child support payments from the fathers of their children. Pat's Family and Medical Leave Act, which gives parents up to twelve weeks of unpaid leave to care for a newborn or adopted baby or to care for a seriously ill relative, passed in the House and Senate but was vetoed by President Bush in 1992. But in February 1993, the bill was again passed in the House and Senate, and it was signed into law by President Bill Clinton. Pat Schroeder was thrilled, especially when the president acknowledged her hard work that led to its passage.

Some bills Congresswoman Schroeder has supported haven't yet

*Pat attends an event of SANE-FREEZE, an organization advocating
a freeze on nuclear weapons, in the mid-1980s.*

become law. One is the Economic Equity Act, which says women must be
paid the same as men doing similar jobs. It would also make sure that if an
elderly husband or wife had to be placed in a nursing home, the spouse at
home would still have enough money to live on.

In 1987, Pat Schroeder's deep concern for the problems faced by the
American family led her to a momentous decision. She decided to run for the
presidency of the United States. Not since Shirley Chisholm threw her hat in
the ring in 1972 had a Democratic woman been a candidate for president.

Pat thought people would support her. She had served in the House of
Representatives for fourteen years. She held important assignments on
the Armed Services Committee and the House Select Committee on
Children, Youth, and Families as well as the House Post Office and
Judiciary committees. Her work as an advocate for men and women in the
military, for cutting unnecessary military spending, and for programs to
help families had earned her great respect among her colleagues and
throughout America.

From the moment she considered running, Pat was firm. "If I do this, if I really run, it has got to be to win." She didn't want to run for president only to lose the election *and* her job in Congress. (If she ran for president, she could not also run for Congress.)

Pat and her staff knew it would be hard to convince the Democrats to nominate her in 1988. It would also be very difficult to raise the millions of dollars necessary for the race. It takes a staggering amount of money to run for president—at least $20 million! And she thought she would have to raise at least $2 million just to prove she had enough support from the people. From early July until late September 1987, Pat was on the campaign trail, making speeches and meeting with people who could donate money to her campaign. She was also trying to get a sense of how the American people felt about electing a woman as president. At first, her chances looked good. Many newspapers and television stations reported that the voters wanted Pat to be president. Magazines such as *Time* and *People* had stories about her. The National Organization for Women raised over $300,000 in one evening for Pat's campaign. And everywhere she went, the crowds were enormous. In one small town in Minnesota, two hundred fifty people were expected to hear Pat talk.

Pat, Scott, Jim, and Jamie in 1988.

Instead, twelve hundred people were waiting when she arrived.

In the fall of 1987, Pat made her decision. She and Jim had studied the situation carefully. So far they had raised $1 million. While that is a lot of money, it was only half the amount they knew they needed *before* the Democrats chose their candidate. And despite the crowds who came to hear her speeches, Pat Schroeder wasn't certain that the American people would elect a woman president that year. So, on September 28, 1987, she faced a large group of supporters in Civic Park in Denver. Pat looked at the expectant faces of those who were eager for her to be the next president of the United States and told them she could not be their candidate. A great moan of disappointment rose up from the crowd. Pat choked up with emotion. "I can't figure out how to run," she said. And then she stopped. She wiped tears from her eyes. "There must be a way, but I haven't figured it out." She was unable to continue. Pat turned to Jim, who was standing behind her, and they embraced.

Some people thought that it was "unmanly" of her to cry. Other critics said they wouldn't want a president who might cry if she had to lead us into war. Pat answered, "I wouldn't want that person to be someone who *doesn't* cry."

Pat's brief run for president in 1987 made her an even stronger member of Congress. Her travels around the country that year showed her how deeply people felt about family issues such as affordable day care for young children, national health care for all Americans, home health care for the elderly, and the right of a woman to decide whether or not to have an abortion.

As the woman who has served longest in Congress, Pat Schroeder is looked upon as a role model by newly elected congresswomen. She has brought many serious issues affecting women and children to the attention of the public and continues to work for laws that will strengthen the American family—whether it is a two-parent family, a single-parent family, or an intergenerational family. Strengthening *all* American families is a top priority for Congresswoman Pat Schroeder. "It is," said Pat, "our country's future that is at stake."

Millicent Fenwick, about 1979.

MILLICENT FENWICK
"We Are All in This Together"

REPUBLICAN OF NEW JERSEY
United States Representative: January 1975–January 1983

When Millicent Fenwick was elected to the House of Representatives in 1974, she was sixty-four years old. This is an age when most people think about slowing down or retiring. But not the feisty Republican from Bernardsville, New Jersey! During the next eight years, this pipe-smoking, elegant, former fashion model would become known throughout the country as the "conscience of the House."

As a member of the House Ethics Committee, Millicent often lambasted her colleagues for their "pork-barrel" spending, a term used when members of Congress try to get as much money as possible for projects such as roads, post offices, and bridges in their districts. Millicent believed that before any taxpayers' money got spent for such projects, the members of Congress ought to show proof that their districts really needed each item.

Millicent was also concerned about how money was spent by candidates running for election. One of her most cherished causes was to change the way money was raised and spent for political campaigns. She was worried because large or rich organizations which had a "special interest" in getting a candidate elected could legally give thousands of dollars to that person's campaign. She knew that "money talks." A candidate who receives lots of money from a special interest group is more likely to vote for bills that favor the money-giver. But no matter how she tried, she was never able to get a bill passed that would put stricter limits on campaign contributions.

Millicent Fenwick practiced what she preached. She set a fine example of how a person can win on a limited budget by announcing her budget at the beginning of election season. And she stuck to it. She spent no more than $22,000 for each of her campaigns for the House of Representatives. She never accepted contributions from special interest groups and did not use her great wealth to "spend" her way into office. Sometimes her opponents agreed not to spend a lot of money, either, but not always.

Some of her colleagues, especially those she criticized, complained that she was a "scold." Cartoonist G. B. Trudeau, whose comic strip "Doonesbury" appears in hundreds of newspapers, created Lacey Davenport, a character based on Congresswoman Fenwick. Lacey Davenport became the humorous symbol of the honest, serious politician bent on reforming her naughty colleagues. Mr. Trudeau often used Millicent's own words in the comic strip. And the congresswoman loved it. She had a ready smile and appreciated a good joke, even at her own expense.

And she liked being in politics.

Once a reporter from the *Newark Evening News* asked if he could tag along with her one day when she was campaigning. They left her home in Bernardsville, New Jersey, at nine in the morning and did not return until nine that evening. During that time she drove through many towns and cities in her district. She made several speeches and even marched in a parade. Millicent did take time out to eat a baloney sandwich, which she had packed to take along. By the day's end, the reporter, probably half the congresswoman's age, was exhausted.

"On the way back into my driveway—I was driving, naturally—" Millicent remembered, "the reporter said, 'You know, this was a perfectly horrible day. How do you stand it? You seem to enjoy it so much.' And I replied, 'Well, that's what politics demands.'

"I put my car into the garage. I saw the taillights of his car going down the driveway. And it was a beautiful autumn night. I looked up at the stars and I thought, 'Do I enjoy it?' And when I reached the door, I thought, 'Yes, I really do enjoy it. Because the answer is that we are all in this together.' "

Millicent Vernon Hammond was born on February 25, 1910. She grew up in a fifty-room house on thirty-three acres of land in Bernardsville, New Jersey. Her mother, Mary, was a descendant of John Stevens, the founder of the Stevens Institute of Technology, a college in Hoboken, New Jersey. Her father, Ogden, was a financier, a person who advises corporations, governments, and wealthy people on how to make money. It seemed as if Millicent was destined for a life of luxury and privilege. Yet her parents believed that wealthy people should spend part of their lives serving others and trying to do good in the world.

"Old-fashioned" words such as *justice, fairness, truth,* and *honesty* would always have great meaning for Millicent. "You don't need a law about fairness," she once said. "And you don't need laws about loving or charity or decency. The trick is to behave responsibly." Millicent believed "that the whole point of government is justice."

When she was just five years old, Millicent, her older sister, Mary, and little brother, Arthur, were left in the care of the staff at their New Jersey mansion. Her parents had traveled by ship to Europe during World War I. They were part of a group of people who were trying to find a way to stop the war.

On the Hammonds' return trip, their ship, the *Lusitania,* was torpedoed by the German navy. Mrs. Hammond got into one of the lifeboats with other women and children. As the sailors were lowering it into the water, the lifeboat tipped over. All of its passengers were tossed into the freezing, swirling waters. Millicent's father jumped into the ocean to try to save his wife. He grabbed onto a piece of wood and hung on until he was rescued, but Mrs. Hammond was never found.

Mr. Hammond remarried a few years later, and Millicent acquired an older stepbrother. Sometimes her new brother bossed her around.

"I was always resistant to authority," she said. "But we had to obey. My stepbrother had given me eight slaps for my eighth birthday. I was so furious that I went upstairs and woke up my father and my stepmother." She paused, and her blue eyes flashed. "It became clear to me, well, it actually took about a week, that my kind of rebellion would not be tolerated." She did not say what punishment she received for barging into her parents' room and tattling on her stepbrother, but whatever it was, she never forgot it.

Millicent often discovered she couldn't have her own way. "When I was very small, I had a donkey. In the autumn of 1914, just before my mother died, there was a hunt. Mary had a little pony, which she rode sidesaddle. I was hoping to join the hunt." So Millicent got her little donkey all fixed up with ribbons wound through his tail and mane. "But then," she says, "they wouldn't let me join them. So I had a tantrum while my sister went off with the coachman." Millicent remembers standing next to her house watching everyone ride off. She stamped her feet and cried. "I had a very bad temper. All of my life, I have had a very bad temper. And I've learned to hold it."

Millicent loved school. At first she went to Miss Nightingale's School in New York City. (Her family always moved to a smaller home in the city during the winter because it took a ton of coal a day to heat the huge house in New Jersey.) Then she attended the Foxcroft School in Virginia. She left it when she was fifteen years old. "Daddy was made ambassador to Spain, and we had to live there." Even though she had no trouble passing all of the exams necessary for graduation from Foxcroft, the headmistress thought Millicent was too young to get a diploma and refused to let her graduate from high school.

Except for the first three months in Spain, when Millicent was enrolled in a convent school, her formal education was over. She never graduated from high school. But she also never gave up learning.

"While I lived in Spain, I used to send to Paris for books . . . and I read all sorts of books: all of Tolstoy, all of Chekhov, all of Turgenev. And that was my education." Millicent also learned to read, write, and speak fluent Spanish, Italian, and French. And she developed a lifelong interest in history and archeology.

Millicent with Hugh and Mary, about 1945.

When Millicent returned to the United States, she took courses at Columbia University, but she never earned a college degree. She also did some modeling for a fashion magazine called *Harper's Bazaar*. (She had a classic model's tall, slim figure and good looks.)

By the time she was nineteen, Millicent had fallen head over heels in love with Hugh Fenwick, a handsome married man. Their romance created a scandal. Shortly after he obtained his divorce in 1934, Millicent and Hugh married. Full of love and adventure, the newlyweds purchased a farm and attempted to raise dairy cows. And within a couple of years, Millicent was the mother of two children, Mary and Hugh.

Neither the farm nor the marriage did well. After four years of marriage, Hugh Fenwick walked out of Millicent's life. He left her with a pile of debts and with two young children to support.

Although she knew that one day she would inherit a great deal of money, at this moment, during the height of the Great Depression in 1938, Millicent Hammond Fenwick was broke. Sadly, she sold the farm and moved back to the family home with Mary and Hugh. While she and her children were allowed to live there, Millicent had to find a way to support herself and her children and pay back the money owed.

Millicent would soon learn how difficult that would be.

"I remember going on a hot, hot summer day to Bonwit Teller [a well-known, posh department store where, in better days, she had shopped]. And suddenly this lovely flow of cool air from the air conditioning came to the downstairs of the store. But I had to climb up that little ladder and up the staircase to the personnel office. Here it was hot and stuffy. Only the customers were permitted to be cool in those days. And what a terrible shock it was to be told that I couldn't get a job as a salesclerk because I had no high school diploma! So I asked for a job as a runner [a person who runs to the storeroom to replace items that have been sold at the counter]. But I couldn't be a runner because I was too old. I was twenty-eight.

"I went out and I thought, 'What can I do? Is there no place in this life for me?'"

Millicent didn't have time to feel sorry for herself. She needed to find a way to earn her living. Fortunately, a friend recommended her for a job as a writer for *Vogue*, an elegant fashion magazine. Although Millicent didn't know very much about writing, she was a willing student. Soon she was writing articles about fashion, travel, people, and places. Sometimes she modeled for the magazine. Later, she even wrote a book. It was called *Vogue's Book of Etiquette*.

During the years she worked at *Vogue*, she paid off all the old debts. She also found time during her busy schedule to serve on the Bernardsville Board of Education.

It was not until 1952 that the money from her trust fund, about $5 million, became available. Now that she was free of the burden of earning a daily living, Millicent continued in the spirit of her family's tradition of working for good causes. She joined the National Association for the Advancement of Colored People (NAACP) and also worked on a commission to study prison reform. Perhaps her favorite organization was the National Council of Christians and Jews. Millicent, who was Christian, devoted her time to this group for more than thirty years. In the 1980s, a rabbi in Summerville, New Jersey, organized a special fund-raising event to honor Millicent's support of Israel and various Jewish causes. The money raised was used to establish the Fenwick Forest in Israel.

Millicent started her political career in 1958, when she became the first woman ever elected to the Bernardsville Borough Council, which makes the laws for the town. However, she broke with one family tradition. The Fenwicks had all been Democrats. Millicent became a Republican. She believed in the Republican party's commitment to fewer government controls over people's lives. "A good Republican," she said in response to a reporter's question, "is as sensitive to the suffering of others as anyone else, but a first reaction would be, 'Let's get together and do something,' not, 'The government must take charge of this.' " She believed that the Democrats wanted the federal government to use our tax money to solve human problems rather than letting people help themselves and each other.

In 1968, Millicent was elected to the New Jersey state legislature. She attracted attention almost immediately, both because she smoked her pipe during the legislative sessions (she almost always carried two little "lady's" pipes, one of which was blue) and because of her humor. During a debate on the Equal Rights Amendment (ERA), an annoyed member of the legislature said, "I always thought that women were meant to be kiss-able, cuddly, and sweet-smelling." This brought a big laugh from the lawmakers. But Millicent got an even bigger laugh when she replied, "That's what I thought of men. And I hope for your sake that you haven't been disappointed as many times as I've been." She was a strong

Millicent in the New Jersey state legislature, about 1971.

supporter of the ERA, which women and men in many states across the country were trying to get passed. (New Jersey was the fourteenth state to vote to ratify the ERA.)

While in the legislature, Millicent worked for prison reform, conservation, help for consumers, and civil rights. When she introduced a bill requiring farmers to provide "portable sanitation" (toilets) to farmworkers, she earned the nickname "Outhouse Millie"!

During her second term, Millicent Fenwick was asked to become head of the Consumer Affairs Commission for her state, so she resigned from the legislature. It was her job to make sure that items people bought were safe, well-made, and fairly priced. People who had complaints about merchandise could complain to her commission.

In 1974, Millicent ran for a seat in the U.S. House of Representatives, and won. First, she was appointed to the Banking, Currency, and Housing Committee, the Ethics Committee, and the Small Business Committee. When she was reelected to Congress she served on the Standards of Official Conduct Committee, the Select Committee on Aging, and later on the Education and Labor Committee, among others. Her accomplishments during her eight years in the House were many. Always concerned with human rights, she helped create the Helsinki Commission, an international group that monitors human rights around the world. The commission studies how different countries treat the people they send to prison and learns which countries put people in jail because they disagree with their government. It then reports its findings. Millicent also worked hard on behalf of consumers (so that when people bought goods, they got what they paid for at a fair price) and for the elderly. Although many laws which Millicent wrote or helped write (such as one to protect consumers) didn't have her name on them, she didn't mind. "I learned that if you want to get something done, just give someone else the credit."

Millicent supported many traditional Republican platforms. She believed in strong family values and introduced bills to help the elderly stay in their own homes instead of being sent to nursing homes. She believed in the spirit of volunteerism. That is, instead of asking the government for help, she wanted people to get together in their own communities to solve their own problems. The congresswoman believed that even children should learn to volunteer in hospitals and nursing homes as part of their education.

Millicent Fenwick always had an open mind. At first she was in favor of America's role in the war in Vietnam. She supported both President Richard Nixon and President Gerald Ford's requests to send military aid to help South Vietnam. (Although American troops had left South Vietnam in March 1973, the fighting continued.) But in February 1975, Congresswomen Millicent Fenwick and Bella Abzug, with six other members of Congress, went to South Vietnam and neighboring Cambodia on a fact-finding mission. They wanted to see if they should approve President Ford's request for more money for military and economic aid to those two countries. Both, it was feared, would soon be taken over by Communist forces. The fact-finding team met with leaders of South Vietnam and Cambodia. They visited people who had been left homeless and without food because of the war. "I have never seen or imagined such human suffering, and the first thought that comes to mind is 'stop the killing,'" Millicent said on her return.

Millicent voted against sending more military aid to either Cambodia or South Vietnam. Instead she voted to send food, clothing, and medicine to the suffering people there. Although she did not want either country to fall to the Communists, she wrote in the *New York Times* that "the lesson here is that it must be their choice—not ours."

In 1982, when one of the senators from New Jersey retired, Millicent Fenwick decided to run for his seat. As the campaign began, she had a huge lead over her Democratic challenger, Frank Lautenberg. Once again, she announced that she would not spend more than $22,000 for her campaign. But Mr. Lautenberg was also very rich, and he decided to spend as much money as he needed to win the race. He used many expensive television commercials to get his message across. He hammered away at Millicent's age (she was now seventy-two) and said she was too old to be a good senator. (Mr. Lautenberg was about thirty years younger than Millicent.) The voters began to listen to him. Too late, Millicent realized that in order to win the Senate race, she would have to spend a lot of money for television ads to answer his charges. When the votes were counted, Mr. Lautenberg had won.

Millicent was crushed. It was the first time in her political career that she had lost an election. "After forty-eight hours of wondering what I should have done, I just decided that the good Lord knows best," she later said. She went back to Bernardsville and volunteered for several community organizations.

In January 1983, President Ronald Reagan phoned Mrs. Fenwick. He asked if she would consider becoming the U.S. ambassador to the United Nations Food and Agriculture Organization (FAO) in Rome, Italy. Her answer, of course, was yes. So at age seventy-three, Millicent Fenwick was once again serving her country.

When she arrived in Rome, she discovered that a Cadillac limousine and a driver came with the job. Immediately, she sent both car and driver away. "You just can't drive up in a big car to an agency that helps the poor," she told a reporter. Instead, she drove her own small Ford sedan. To save on hotel bills, Millicent lived with a friend until she found a suitable apartment. As she began work on attacking the enormous problems of world hunger, she did so in a very humble way: by studying the people who were to receive help and listening to what kind of help they wanted. "We can't do things *for* people. We must do things *with* people."

When a reporter interviewed her in her office in Rome, she said that she wanted her organization to help the very poorest farmers in the very poorest countries try to survive. She explained how important it was to give farmers tools they could really use. "You can't barge in with a tractor. It's not going to do him any good." A very poor farmer would be more content to trade in a wooden plow for a metal one instead. Millicent believed her job was much more than "feeding the hungry." It was to make people self-reliant.

Millicent retired from the FAO in 1987 and went back home to Bernardsville, New Jersey. As she thought about her life and where it has taken her, she said, "I'm very much in favor of people doing all they can and not giving up. Life will hand all of us its tough little moments. But the mind is like a muscle. You have to keep using it." Millicent Fenwick died at age eighty-two in September 1992.

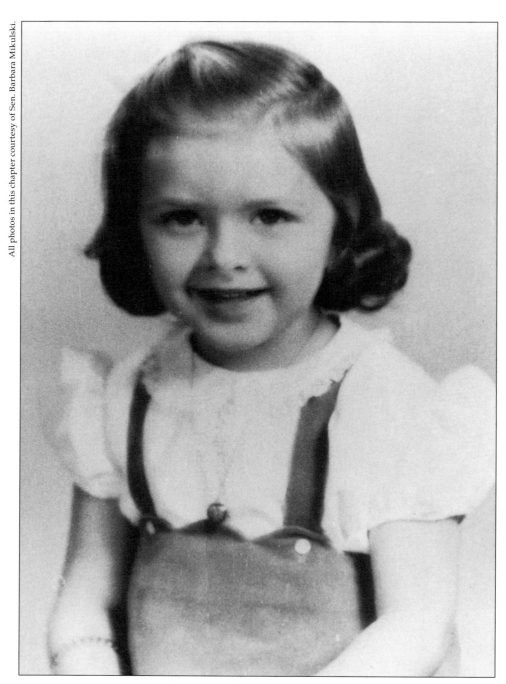

Barbara Mikulski, about age five.

BARBARA MIKULSKI
"The Baltimore Scrapper"

DEMOCRAT OF MARYLAND
United States Representative: January 1977–January 1987
United States Senator: January 1987–Present

It was "the Road" that put Barbara Mikulski on her own road to a career in politics back in 1968. This wasn't just any old road. It was a sixteen-lane superhighway that was going to be built smack-dab in the middle of the Fells Point section of East Baltimore. If that happened, the first neighborhood in Baltimore where African-Americans owned their own homes would have been bulldozed out of existence.

Barb Mikulski, the great-granddaughter of Polish immigrants, joined the fight against "the Road." She had grown up in Highlandtown, one of the many bustling ethnic neighborhoods in East Baltimore. She had lived on one of its winding cobblestone streets famous for its row houses, each with identical scrubbed white marble steps leading up to identical front doors.

Barb knew that strong neighborhoods were important in a large city, and to slice up Fells Point would have meant sudden death to a vibrant neighborhood. She joined SCAR (Southeast Council Against the Road) to fight the politicians supporting the construction. These politicians, Barb said, "were out of touch with what the people really wanted. They were like dinosaurs doing the polka."

It didn't take long before Barb Mikulski became one of the key opponents of the highway. And it didn't take long before people began calling this short (four-foot, eleven-inch), stocky organizer, "the Baltimore Scrapper." At one rally, she told supporters, "We didn't let the British take Fells Point; we didn't let termites take Fells Point; and we're not going to let the State Roads Commission take Fells Point!" Her message got people from all over the city to join forces to stop the superhighway. In less than two years, the politicians backed off. SCAR won its fight. And Barbara Mikulski had become known as a woman who could get things done. She was eager to help organize citizens for other community projects, and there was plenty to keep her busy.

She found the local library in one neighborhood so limited that "once a kid read the Nancy Drew series, she peaked there." Along with other dedicated people, Barb worked to expand the library's hours and add more books. Another time, Barbara learned that a neighborhood school needed a program for students with dyslexia, a disability that causes reading and math problems. She helped people get the program. "We organized on what people's needs were," Barbara said. (This kind of political work is known as "grass-roots organizing.") Through her work, Barbara became a real force among the people of Baltimore.

In 1971, she decided to run for a seat on the city council, which is the elected group of citizens who make the city's laws. To run as a candidate on either the Republican or Democratic ticket, a person needs to be endorsed (approved) by his or her party. Each neighborhood or district has its own Republican or Democratic club which endorses candidates. But Barb soon discovered it was often hard for a newcomer, especially a woman, to be accepted by the local club members (who were mostly older men). Although there were women appointed to the club, their role seemed to be mostly stamping and stuffing envelopes during campaigns and holding potluck suppers to raise money. The men had always picked the candidates to run for public office. So far, they had always chosen men. "If I waited to be a member of the local Democratic club, I would still be cooking sauerkraut at the church supper," Barbara said.

Not surprisingly, the Democratic club endorsed a man for the city council seat. So Barbara Mikulski took her campaign to the people. More than enough registered Democratic voters signed her petition to run, and Barb got her name placed on the primary ballot. She beat her Democratic opponent in the primary and defeated her Republican opponent in the November 1971 election. She was able to do this because she had built up a "tremendous reservoir of good will in the community and people were willing to volunteer for me." The campaign took a lot of hard work on her part, too. "I knocked on fifteen thousand doors that summer, wore out five pairs of shoes, and got mugged by fourteen Chihuahuas!" Her ready wit captured the hearts of her constituents, but her hard work won her the election.

Barbara Mikulski has several traits which make people want to vote for her. She has boundless energy, a willingness to listen to the needs of people, and a sense of humor. She has a deep-down love for both her native city of Baltimore and for her country. To this day, she admits that when she hears an old recording of Kate Smith singing "God Bless America," it's "a three-Kleenex affair for me."

Her patriotism grew out of a childhood nurtured by strong family and church ties. Barbara Ann Mikulski was born on July 20, 1936, in a Polish working-class neighborhood bounded on one side by another working-class neighborhood known as "Little Italy." Farther on were areas with Ukrainians, Greeks, Germans, and other first- and second-generation Americans of European heritage. Among the tidy row houses were warehouses and restaurants, fish markets and vegetable stands, and imposing Catholic churches and schools. Many men earned their livings as steelworkers, shopkeepers, and shipbuilders, or as stevedores who unloaded huge shipments of goods along the docks.

Barbara's parents, William and Christine Eleanor Mikulski, ran a little grocery store called Willy's Market across the street from their house. Nearby was Mikulski's Bakery, owned by Barb's aunt and uncle. The neighborhood was a place where everybody knew everybody else, and where grownups watched out for everyone's children.

Until America entered World War II in 1941, most people in East Baltimore spoke not only English but a foreign language as well. "So I spoke Polish from the time I was a little kid until I was about six," Barbara said.

By 1942, all that had changed. With the United States at war against

Germany, Italy, and Japan, many people were either ashamed or afraid to speak a foreign language, especially in public places. Since she was just a child, it was easy for Barbara to switch to English. "Everybody wanted to prove that they were Americans."

As the nation looked for ways to help America win the war against Nazi Germany and its allies, Barbara and her friends found they could help, too.

"My mother and father wanted me to know that there was a war going on and we all had to make sacrifices." Every week, Barbara would take a quarter from her spending money and buy a war stamp at school. Each stamp was about the same size as a regular postage stamp, only it could not be used to mail a letter. The stamps were pasted into a booklet. When a person had saved seventy-five stamps ($18.75), she or he turned the booklet in at a bank or post office in exchange for a $25 war bond. The money from the sale of the stamps helped the United States government to pay for the war. In return, the government agreed to pay back the money with interest in ten years. Buying war bonds got Barbara into a lifelong habit of saving.

On Saturdays, Barb and her friends scoured the neighborhood, collecting materials for the war effort. "I had a little red wagon, and with the other kids, I'd pick up newspapers and other recyclables and take them to the depot."

As the war continued, it became necessary for certain goods to be rationed. All families had books of ration coupons that allowed them to buy small amounts of sugar, meat, and butter. Each time a rationed item was bought, the customer would give a coupon to the grocer. Barbara's job on weekends was to sort out the coupons the customers had given her parents.

But the war didn't keep Barbara from having a regular childhood. She and her friends rode their bikes after school and played sandlot softball. Because she was the shortest child and not well coordinated, Barbara wasn't good at games such as "double-Dutch" or jacks. She found another way to be a leader.

The Mikulskis had a big double garage but only one car. Barb turned the empty half into a little theater and put on plays. All the neighborhood children wanted to be in them, and those who didn't get a part came to watch. "I wrote the plays; I directed the plays; I starred in the plays," she said. She had such fun doing this that she thought one day she might become a famous playwright.

When Barbara was nine years old, her aunt gave her a chemistry set. It came with a little book of experiments a child could do at home in the kitchen or basement. Barbara set about trying out every one, and chemistry became one of her many hobbies.

After seeing the movie "Madame Curie," the story of a Polish woman scientist who won Nobel prizes in chemistry and physics, Barbara began to realize just how many career opportunities there were for women. "I was from a strong ethnic family where women helped run family businesses. And I went to all-girls' Catholic schools. So I saw women who ran businesses; I had nuns in school who were teachers; and I was surrounded by women who were very competent."

Her favorite after-school activity was the Girl Scouts. Scouting gave Barbara a chance to learn new skills as she worked on earning her badges. And there were many ways for her to test herself and gain confidence. To this day, Barbara carries the Girl Scout pledge in her wallet. "When I give speeches, even to Chamber of Commerce groups, I say, 'Do you know what I think the United States Senate ought to be doing?' And I whip out my little yellow card with the green letters and talk about being honest, being cheerful, and so on. Of course, everyone laughs. But they all know that that's really a code of conduct." The Girl Scouts of America have made Barbara Mikulski a lifetime member!

Barbara polished her natural talent for public speaking when she joined the debate team in high school. She remembers debating the merits of the Republican and Democratic presidential candidates, General Dwight D. Eisenhower and Adlai E. Stevenson, in 1952. She spoke for Stevenson. Even though the Republican, Eisenhower, became president that year, Barbara decided then and there she would always be a Democrat.

When Barbara graduated from high school, she considered becoming a nun. But she realized that she had a rebellious nature and decided that the strict discipline of a religious order wasn't right for her. Instead, she became a social worker. She graduated from Mount St. Agnes College in Baltimore and then the University of Maryland. She began her career with the Associated Catholic Charities in Baltimore and later worked for the Baltimore Department of Social Services. She was on her way to becoming a fine administrator when she met up with Sister Mary Elizabeth, a feisty nun who encouraged Barbara to work to change the lives of the poor through education and the electoral process. Sister Mary Elizabeth had started her own school in a poor area of Baltimore where many black people lived. She encouraged people to work for change by electing public officials who would listen to them. Barbara started to volunteer with Sister Mary Elizabeth and other civil rights workers to get people in that area registered to vote. At the same time, Barbara was politically active through her work to stop "the Road." It was a short step from these activities to the city council in 1971.

In 1976, while Barbara was still a city council member, she saw a chance to do more for the people of her district. The congressman from Maryland's Third District had announced he would give up his House seat. Barbara decided to run for Congress.

Barb Mikulski wasn't the only one who wanted that job. She was going to have to beat five men in the Democratic primary, and it wouldn't be easy. Her congressional district included not only her own working-class neighborhood (where she was popular), but also some swanky suburban sections where not many people knew the Baltimore Scrapper. She took stock of herself and decided she'd have to do something about her appearance. The truth was that Barbara Mikulski needed to go on a diet. She was simply too fat. So under a doctor's supervision, she went on a nutritious and balanced diet and also exercised on a cycle. And the pounds began to come off. By November 1976, Barbara had defeated her five opponents in the primary and the Republican in the general election—and she'd lost fifty pounds.

For the next ten years, Barbara Mikulski threw herself into her work as a member of the House of Representatives. Among her committee assignments was Merchant Marines and Fisheries, an excellent place for her to help the Port of Baltimore, where thousands of her constituents worked. She secured money for an important Baltimore port-dredging project and successfully sponsored a bill to preserve coastal areas while allowing for some development as well. Preserving the environment became one of her goals.

One of her proudest moments was when the 1984 Child Abuse Act became law. Barbara was one of its main sponsors. This law helps abused children all over the country. It requires that doctors and other health care workers report abuse when they suspect it. She also worked hard to pass the Equal Rights Amendment. Her own state of Maryland was the eighteenth state to ratify the amendment, but in the end, it didn't pass.

Barbara is deeply concerned with issues that affect women, children, and the elderly. She supports the right of a woman to choose to have an abortion. She has introduced bills in the House to provide more funds for child care, health care for the elderly, and assistance for displaced home-makers (women who are suddenly left without any means of support because their husbands have either died or divorced them). She has also fought to keep hospital costs down.

One of Barb's achievements especially pleased her Maryland constituents. Her support helped Baltimore get a beautiful new base-ball stadium!

In 1986, Barbara Mikulski decided to run for the Senate. If she won, it would be the first time a Democratic woman became a senator without following her husband into office. Although she wouldn't be the first woman to serve in both the House and Senate—Margaret Chase Smith was—she would be the only one to do so without filling a seat held by a husband. (Margaret Chase Smith took over her husband's seat in the House after he died.)

Barb's plan was risky. To campaign for the Senate, she'd have to give up her seat in the House of Representatives. She knew she could easily win

Barbara campaigns for the Senate.

another term in the House. But if she lost the Senate race, she'd be out of politics. All the people in a state vote for senators. Could the Baltimore Scrapper win support throughout Maryland?

Some people complained that Barb didn't look "senatorial." How could she? Of the one hundred senators, ninety-eight were men! Nancy Kassebaum, Republican from Kansas, and Paula Hawkins, Republican from Florida, were the only women in the Senate. (Paula Hawkins was not reelected in 1986.) Other people remarked on Barbara's clothes. They weren't stylish enough; her eyeglasses gave her an owlish look; her hair style was dowdy; and so on. Although Barbara knew that her looks had nothing to do with her performance as a lawmaker, she listened to her critics. Since she couldn't do anything about her height or her sex, she concentrated on her appearance. (Many men who run for public office also work to improve their looks.)

An adviser to presidential candidates showed Barbara how to use new makeup so she would look better on television. And Barbara bought rimless, low-glare eyeglasses. She took the advice of fashion experts and purchased an up-to-date wardrobe. Barbara thought this was all great fun, although it may have been hard to go back on a low-calorie diet once again. None of these things changed the "essential Barbara." They just softened the rough East Baltimore edges.

The race for the Senate was the toughest campaign of her life. This time she ran against another woman, Republican Linda Chavez. President Reagan backed the Republican candidate, and all over the nation, Republicans were being swept into office. But not in Maryland. Barbara Mikulski won with over 60 percent of the vote.

Overnight, Barbara became a national celebrity. She said she had proved it was possible for "someone who is not male, wealthy, or possessed of good looks, who is fiercely outspoken, to take a place among the wealthy white males who traditionally dominate the Senate."

Once Senator Barbara Mikulski got to work (she was given the desk that had belonged to President Harry Truman when he was a senator), she wasted little time. She had promised the people of Maryland that she would be concerned about all their problems, and she wanted to keep her word. She secured an assignment on the Small Business Committee, where she helped farmers and fishermen by getting more money for research in agriculture and for oyster beds. (Oysters are one of Maryland's big seafood industries.) She sits on the Appropriations Committee, which oversees every aspect of government spending. Barb saw to it that her state received money for mass transit (buses and trains). She is also on the Labor and Human Resources Committee, where bills which deal with welfare reform legislation begin.

Barbara Mikulski is dedicated to improving our national health care, especially for the elderly. She has co-sponsored a bill to provide the elderly with home health care and nursing home care insurance, and in

1987 wrote a law which sets high standards for home health care and nursing homes. She wants to make sure that all women, young or elderly, get their fair share of health care, too. In 1990, she convinced the National Institutes of Health to create an Office on Women's Health. It had been revealed that much research into illness focused on men's health problems and not those of women.

In 1992, Senator Mikulski ran for a second term in the Senate. This time, she won with more than 70 percent of the vote. Her fellow Democrats in the Senate rewarded her victory by appointing her assistant floor leader. Barbara is one of four Democratic senators who have this job. The assistant floor leader and the floor leader meet directly with the president to discuss legislation, and with leaders in the House to iron out differences in bills which both houses pass. In addition to her other duties, Barbara is the chairperson of the Subcommittee on Aging, which is part of the Labor and Human Resources Committee. She is also a member of the Senate Ethics Committee, which investigates charges of wrongdoing by other senators.

Barbara speaks during a Senate campaign.

Barbara visits a Head Start center.

Senator Barbara Mikulski still thinks of herself as a good Girl Scout. "You know what?" she said, "I'm still working on badges, only now it's called the National Health Insurance Act or it's called the Women's Health Equity Act. So instead of Girl Scout badges, I work on legislation. It's all the same thing. You do your homework, you get very personally involved, and you've got to construct solutions."

Nancy Kassebaum at age four.

NANCY KASSEBAUM
Citizen Legislator

REPUBLICAN OF KANSAS

United States Senator: January 1979–Present

The week before Nancy Jo Landon's fourth birthday, her father, Alfred (Alf) Landon, was nominated by the Republican party to be its candidate for president of the United States.

Although he lost the 1936 election to Franklin Delano Roosevelt, a Democrat, Alf Landon remained an important Republican politician in Kansas, where he was governor from 1933 to 1937. So politics were part of Nancy's daily life. It was not unusual for her and her younger brother, Jack, to listen to the grownups discuss important issues around the dinner table. Sometimes, after they were upstairs in bed, they listened to the grownups' conversation through the heating vents. Nancy recalled that when she was in grade school, she used to go around handing out campaign literature before each election. Still, she never dreamed she'd become a politician herself.

Nancy grew up just outside the city limits of Topeka, Kansas. "We lived on a working farm. I can remember my grandmother hanging the cottage cheese [wrapped in cheesecloth] on the line to drip. And we churned butter and canned a lot." Dorothy, the Kansas-born heroine of *The Wizard of Oz*, would have felt very comfortable at Nancy's home.

Summer was a time for Nancy and her brother to explore the countryside, swim in the Kawl River, and spend a lot of time playing on its sandbars. But sometimes she and her friend Betty Carmine, who lived down the road, had to find ways to keep busy during the long, scorching summer days. "Of course, during the 1940s," Nancy said, "there was no air conditioning or television. So we just closed up the house and turned on the fan and read or played games." When they got bored, the children played with the many pets that Nancy always had—birds, dogs, cats, a raccoon, and her Shetland pony.

"I had a cocker spaniel for many years. Her name was Gopy." Nancy had named her for the *"Grand Old Party"*—which is a nickname for the Republican party. Raising baby rabbits also kept Nancy and Jack busy. "The haying machine would sometimes run over a rabbit's nest [and kill the mother rabbit]." The children would care for the babies until they were able to go out on their own.

To earn spending money one summer, Nancy, Betty, and Jack ran a pet shop. They raised canaries and parakeets and had a lively business. Another summer, the children set up a flower stand.

The excitement of national elections spilled over into Nancy's games. In 1940, President Roosevelt ran against a Republican, Wendell Willkie. Nancy was cheering Mr. Willkie on. It was Nancy's idea that she and Betty conduct a poll. She wanted to see how many people who drove down her road were going to vote for Mr. Willkie and how many for Mr. Roosevelt. "We made a huge dandelion chain and strung it across the road. My friend stood on one side of the road and I on the other. And we'd ask the people who stopped, 'Willkie or Roosevelt?' Then we'd mark down their responses. People stopped because they were amused by us." Although the results of her poll showed Mr. Willkie was in the lead, to Nancy's disappointment, President Roosevelt was reelected.

Nancy and Betty played the piano and were required to practice a lot. One day, when they were about thirteen, they agreed that they were tired of practicing. "So we decided to run away," Nancy said. To their amazement, both sets of parents said, "OK." In fact, Betty's father drove the girls to the train station in Topeka.

"Well," said Nancy, "you can imagine right there that that was enough to give us pause. We had no idea where we were going. We thought that there would be a great hue and cry. So we bravely got out of the car, and Betty's father drove off."

Left to themselves in the cavernous railroad station, the girls weren't quite brave enough to buy a ticket and get on a train. It wasn't long before Nancy sheepishly called home and asked someone to pick them up.

Until she was in college, Nancy never gave much thought to what she would do with her life. She graduated from the University of Kansas in 1954 and earned a master's degree in diplomatic history from the University of Michigan two years later. "When I thought about a career at all, it was in terms of going into the foreign service."

But Nancy did not test her first career aspirations. She happily chose marriage instead of a career. She had met Phil Kassebaum, a young lawyer, while still in graduate school. They were married in 1955 and moved to a suburb of Wichita, Kansas, where Nancy and Phil bought a radio station. By 1962, Nancy was the mother of four children: John, born in 1957; Linda, 1959; Richard, 1960; and William, 1962.

Nancy plunged into the activities that many mothers of young children do. She baked cookies for class parties and was active in the PTA, 4-H, and other organizations that promoted good citizenship and education. She loved to garden, and, of course, she always volunteered to help elect Republican candidates.

Nancy was concerned about how well the local schools were educating children. So in 1973, she became a candidate herself for the first time. She won a place on the local school board. She was forty-one years old.

Many people began to think that Alf Landon's daughter had inherited his political savvy. (Her father, who had never run for an elective office after he left the governor's mansion, was still considered the head of the Kansas Republican party. He was consulted by Republicans from all over the country until he was well into his nineties. He died a month after his one hundredth birthday.) As her children grew up, it seemed natural for Nancy to become more deeply involved in Kansas politics, both on local and state levels. In 1974, while still on the school board, she was appointed to the Kansas Governmental Ethics Commission and to the Kansas Commission for the Humanities (a committee that set standards for teaching English, languages, and history in the public schools).

President Reagan visits Alf Landon to celebrate his one hundredth birthday in 1987.

One area of Nancy's life was not going well. In 1977, Nancy and Phil decided to separate. With her children nearing adulthood, Nancy was free to move to Washington, D.C., where she joined the staff of James B. Pearson, the Republican senator from Kansas.

Shortly after Nancy started her job, the senator decided not to seek reelection. For many months Nancy mulled over the possibility of running for Mr. Pearson's seat. By now she had several years of experience serving on committees for the state. In the time she'd been in Washington, she'd found that she loved being in the thick of politics. However, Nancy was not the only Republican who wanted the job as senator. Nine men entered the primary race with her.

Her dad, however, opposed Nancy's plans. In fact, he confided to friends that he didn't think his daughter could win. He thought that her upcoming divorce would become a campaign issue.

Alf Landon was wrong. Nancy's divorce did not become an issue, and she beat her closest opponent in the primary by thirteen thousand votes. She had used her full name—Nancy Landon Kassebaum—in her campaign. This made people aware that she was the daughter of one of the most important and well-respected Republicans in the state. Her message to the voters was that problems could be solved by a thoughtful, reasonable person like herself. Nancy's sincerity was the decisive factor in her victory.

In the fall of 1978, she faced the Democratic challenger. As in the primary, Nancy campaigned as a "citizen legislator." She frankly told the voters that she didn't have a whole lot of political experience, but that she could substitute a good dose of common sense for any lack of political know-how. Voters all across Kansas appreciated her soft-spoken, earnest manner. They were willing to trust this diminutive (five-foot, two-inch tall) woman to represent the people of Kansas. Thousands of Republican women worked on her campaign because they were thrilled to have such an outstanding female candidate. She beat her male opponent after a hard fight.

Nancy Landon Kassebaum became the first female senator in U.S. history who had not followed her husband into office. (Although Margaret Chase Smith was elected to the Senate in her own right, she was originally elected to Congress to fill her husband's seat in the House of Representatives.) For the first two years of Nancy's term, she was the only woman among one hundred senators! (In 1981, she was joined by Senator Paula Hawkins, a Republican from Florida who served until 1987. In 1986, Barbara Mikulski, a Democrat from Maryland, was elected to the Senate. Four more women senators were elected in 1992, the year Senator Mikulski was reelected.)

Alf Landon was delighted that he had been wrong. "It's the thrill of a lifetime," he said. And he predicted, "She'll be a good senator."

When Nancy arrived in Washington, she proved that the voters had elected more than a famous name. Other senators soon recognized her as a serious lawmaker who could think for herself. Nancy also became known for her willingness to look at all sides of a problem and for her ability to listen attentively. Her personal, homey touch carries over to her staff. In addition to writing letters to answer the questions of constituents, they will often telephone people who need immediate answers.

Nancy is not the sort of person who seeks publicity. But when President Ronald Reagan selected her as a special observer to the national elections in El Salvador in 1982, she became the chief spokesperson for the American delegation. Almost every night for a week, Nancy appeared on television to tell the American people what was going on in that Central American nation. The people back in Kansas were thrilled to see that their senator had become an expert on foreign affairs.

Nancy returned to Washington and reported her findings to President Reagan. She told him the Salvadoran military had too much power in its country's government, and that the election she had observed was not fairly conducted. As a member of the Senate Foreign Relations Committee, Nancy worked out a compromise with Democratic colleagues on a bill for military aid for El Salvador. It provided money, but far less than the president had asked for.

No matter how hard Nancy worked during her first term in the Senate, she still had to remind her father that she really knew what she was talking about. Once, when he was pressing her to pay attention to the views of the attorney general of Kansas on an important issue, Nancy said, "Dad, I know more about it than he does!" That was when Alf stopped giving his daughter advice. "She doesn't take it anyway, unless she likes it. And she's been right so many times that I've stopped worrying."

Nancy enjoys working behind the scenes to reach a compromise on complex bills. (Such "give and take" is part of the democratic process.) She knows when to give in on issues and when to stand fast. Nancy believes that because they take care of their families, women are "more used to having to work out compromises than men are."

Nancy visits with students in western Kansas.

By nature, Nancy is not pushy; she admits that she is not a good debater; and she doesn't have a dozen quick jokes up her sleeve. Instead, her strength lies in her ability to see both sides of a question.

Senator Kassebaum's work continues even when she goes home. She is recognized everywhere. "You know, even when I'm at the grocery store, people will come up to me and talk about issues." Sometimes this is frustrating to Nancy, who likes nothing better than to slip into a pair of blue jeans once she gets home. She likes to putter in her garden or to visit with her grandchildren after a full day's work.

At her office, Nancy is efficient and organized. She meets with her staff to discuss which upcoming bills will be voted on and makes decisions as to how she will vote; reads reports on issues her aides have researched; reads and answers letters from her constituents; meets with other members of Congress to discuss important legislation; meets with individuals and groups of people from Kansas; and attends committee meetings.

Nancy has served on the Banking, Housing, and Urban Affairs Committee, the Budget Committee, and the Foreign Relations Committee. She has been chairwoman of the Foreign Relations Committee's Subcommittee on African Affairs and the Aviation Subcommittee of the Commerce, Science, and Transportation Committee. Currently she is the ranking member (the member most senior, next to the chairperson) on the Labor and Human Resources Committee and the International Economic Policy, Trade, Oceans, and Environment Subcommittee of the Foreign Relations Committee. She also serves on the Indian Affairs Committee and the Joint Committee on the Organization of Congress.

In 1986, when Ronald Reagan was president, she urged him to place special sanctions on South Africa such as not trading certain goods with that country. She hoped the sanctions would force South Africa to stop its ill-treatment of its black citizens. She was disappointed when the president didn't take her advice. But she worked with Republican senators to get the sanctions approved.

As chairwoman of the Aviation Subcommittee during her first term, Nancy helped develop updated and safer traffic control procedures for the airlines. And her plans to save the Rock Island Railroad, which is very important to Kansas, were approved. Nancy's service to the people of Kansas and the country was rewarded by the voters. They sent her back to the Senate in 1984 and again in 1990.

Nancy is a staunch Republican but maintains an independent streak. When many women's organizations all over America were urging her *not* to vote to approve Clarence Thomas to the Supreme Court in 1991, she stuck by President Bush and voted with the Republicans for Mr. Thomas's appointment. Yet, she has broken ranks with the official Republican platform over several key issues. She supported passage of the Equal Rights Amendment and supports the right of women to choose to have an abortion. The Republican party opposes these stands. Although she was

Nancy meets with children outside a feeding camp in Somalia in 1992.

against a Republican move to approve a constitutional amendment allowing prayer in public schools, Nancy voted to permit schoolchildren to
observe a moment of silence each day so that those who wished to pray
could. Senator Kassebaum defended her independent views when she
said, "I don't think people should be running for office if they don't have
their own views."

In the summer of 1992, Senator Kassebaum traveled to the African
country of Somalia to see for herself the terrible effects of war and famine
there. She was the first high-ranking U.S. official to visit Somalia in two
years. When she returned to the United States, she alerted reporters to the
dire conditions of the Somalian people. Senator Kassebaum called for
armed UN security forces to protect food shipments to the Somalians.
In November 1992, President George Bush sent U.S. marines to help in

this effort. France and Germany also sent troops to deliver food and medical supplies.

Nancy finds "dealing with people" to be the best part of her job. She said, "There are so many things I wouldn't have known if I hadn't come across these people." When one of her constituents told her of the need for research on little-known diseases, Nancy introduced the Orphan Drug Bill, which became law in 1981. That constituent had Huntington's disease, a serious illness, but one which affects only a few thousand people each year. The Orphan Drug Bill gives pharmaceutical companies funds to work on experimental drugs that might cure rare diseases, such as Huntington's. Because it is very expensive to do drug research, pharmaceutical companies need to know they won't lose money by developing a drug that not many people need to buy. When the federal government provides money for research into rare diseases, the drug companies can then set a price on the new drug that patients can afford.

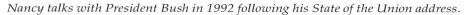

Nancy talks with President Bush in 1992 following his State of the Union address.

Nancy takes great pleasure in knowing she has truly helped thousands of people.

There are times when Nancy doesn't take credit for what she's done, as when she convinced other Republican senators to vote for sanctions against South Africa. "Sometimes you're working behind the scenes and sometimes you're working out front [as with the Orphan Drug Bill]. I've always said that you shouldn't care so much if your name was attached to something if indeed your aim was accomplished." Yet she admitted that not getting one's name on a bill can sometimes "be a bitter pill to swallow, especially if you know you had a major hand in how a bill turns out."

For her third term in the Senate, Nancy Landon Kassebaum has a clear goal: she wants Congress to pass a law that will ensure that all Americans receive health care. In the summer of 1992, Nancy and several other Republicans in the Senate, along with several Democrats in the House, introduced a bill to provide a basic health care plan for all Americans. To pay for this medical care, the government would take one percent of the money in the Social Security fund. If people wanted more than a basic health care package, then they would have to pay for it through their place of employment. Senator Kassebaum's bill would require that all companies offer health care coverage.

"I tell you," she said, "that if I finish this third term and feel that I have made a difference in health care issues, I will count that as something I'm the most proud of."

Geraldine Ferraro in 1992.

GERALDINE FERRARO
"There Are No Doors We Can't Unlock"

DEMOCRAT OF NEW YORK
United States Representative: January 1979–January 1985

"Ladies and gentlemen of the convention—my name is Geraldine Ferraro. I stand before you to proclaim tonight: America is a land where dreams can come true for all of us. . . .

"My fellow citizens, I proudly accept your nomination for vice-president of the United States. . . .

"Tonight the daughter of a woman whose highest goal was a future for her children talks to our nation's oldest party about a future for us all. . . .

"Tonight, the daughter of an immigrant from Italy has been chosen to run for president in the new land my father came to love."

Oops! For just a brief moment, Gerry Ferraro's eyes skipped over the word "vice" on the teleprompter, but she didn't realize it, so she went right on with her acceptance speech. No one seemed to care that she made a tiny mistake that evening.

The ten thousand women and men at the Democratic National Convention in San Francisco knew they were witnessing a historic moment. On the night of July 19, 1984, the first woman ever chosen by a major political party to run for vice-president was speaking to them and the nation. The Democrats had picked Geraldine Ferraro to be the running mate of presidential candidate Walter "Fritz" Mondale. Mr. Mondale believed that her candidacy would encourage large numbers of both Democratic and Republican women to vote for the Democratic ticket.

They hoped to win back many of those who had voted for Republicans Ronald Reagan and George Bush in 1980.

While thousands cheered wildly inside the convention hall with cries of "GER-RY! GER-RY! GER-RY!" millions of people across the nation sat glued to their TV sets, watching and listening.

Several times during her speech, Gerry mentioned her mother, seventy-nine-year-old Antonetta Ferraro. Mrs. Ferraro was watching her daughter on television in her apartment in Queens, New York. Friends, relatives, and dozens of reporters shared this moment with her. Tears rolled down Antonetta Ferraro's cheeks several times during Gerry's speech, and she applauded every few seconds. "I wish I had four hands," Mrs. Ferraro said to her visitors.

Antonetta Ferraro knew better than anyone the challenges Gerry had faced throughout her childhood. She was proud that these experiences had helped her daughter become a fiery and compassionate champion of other Americans.

In 1943, when Geraldine Anne Ferraro was eight, her father died. She remembers the next four years as "probably the worst years of my life. My

Gerry and a cousin in 1942.
Gerry and schoolmates in 1948.

father died very suddenly. We were having dinner with him one Sunday night, and the next morning he was dead of a heart attack." Gerry's mother had no job skills and little schooling. She had to find a way to support her two children and herself.

Just four months later, Gerry was sent to a Catholic boarding school. Her mother had given up their lovely home in Newburgh, New York, and found work in the Bronx. Gerry's older brother, Carl, was already attending a military academy, and relatives continued to pay his tuition. Mrs. Ferraro rented a tiny one-bedroom apartment in the South Bronx. During the day she worked long hours at home, crocheting beads onto dresses for a dress factory. At night, she worked as a sales clerk.

At boarding school, Gerry hid her true feelings from everyone. But at night, when she was alone in bed, she wept. "I used to cry myself to sleep every night because I missed my father so." Within a few months, she became gravely ill.

Gerry's mother rushed to the school and brought her home. The doctor concluded that the shock of her father's death had made Gerry ill. She was suffering from a blood disorder that left her very weak. Gerry stayed at home for many months until she became strong enough to attend classes again.

This time her mother sent her to a Catholic day school just five blocks from their apartment. Gerry could come home for lunch each day for the special diet she needed. Twice a week, her mother took her to a doctor in Manhattan who gave her vitamin shots. It was two years before Gerry was cured.

"With that," said Gerry, "my other life began." Now she attended Marymount School, a Catholic boarding school in Tarrytown, New York. She loved it there. Still, she recalled, "I was so lonely." Besides being homesick for her mother, Gerry was still grieving for her dad. And while other girls had families who paid their school fees, Gerry was a scholarship student. "I learned very, very young that nobody was going to buy my future. I had to *earn* it. I had to be the best in order to get scholarships."

Yet Gerry's drive to be successful has always been tempered with a concern for others who are struggling. "It's probably my Catholic upbringing. I believe that we have an obligation to each other. I know that if I hadn't had help, I would not have achieved."

Gerry went on to Marymount College in Manhattan, an easy subway ride from her home in the Bronx. "I didn't want to be away from my mother anymore. I wanted to be home." Although she had planned to study journalism, her mother convinced her to become a teacher. She majored in English, and when she graduated from Marymount College in 1956, Gerry had earned enough education credits to teach school.

"I loved it. I taught elementary school in Queens for five years," she said. Still, teaching wasn't quite what Gerry wanted. She decided to become a lawyer. Even though she taught all day and ran the after-school program until five o'clock, Gerry Ferraro studied law at night at Fordham University School of Law in New York City. When she entered law school in 1957, there were only five women in her class of over four hundred. By the time she graduated in 1960, there were only two!

Gerry finished law school before getting married. "I'd met my husband when I was nineteen. I was dating John's best friend, and we used to double date." Six years after they met, John and Gerry married.

Although it was very unusual in 1960, Geraldine Ferraro kept her family name instead of taking her husband's. She did this to honor her mother, whose strength had kept the family together. "Remember," her mother had often told her, "*Ferro* means iron. You can bend it, but you can't break it." John Zaccaro, who is a lawyer and real estate developer, is in some ways a traditional Italian husband, but he did not mind having his wife keep her name. However, he didn't want Gerry to work outside of the home.

The new bride convinced her husband otherwise. She remembered how unprepared her own mother had been to support a family. They agreed Gerry would stay home until the youngest child went to school. Then she would go back to work.

In 1961, Donna was born. Two more children followed—John, Jr., in

1964 and Laura in 1966. Gerry did not return to work until 1974, when Laura was eight.

Geraldine Ferraro spent those years when her children were small volunteering with other young mothers in her church and her community in Queens. They put on plays and held bake sales to raise money for a nearby Catholic hospital. She volunteered her time as an attorney in family court. "I did pro bono [free] work for women and children who had been abused," she said. And she also volunteered in her children's school, helping with arts and crafts. "You know," she said, "when you think about women who stay home, they do an awful lot of work as volunteers, and they work hard for their children, too."

It was during this period that Gerry discovered a talent for organizing. Each summer she and her friends took their children to vacation homes at Pear Harbor on the Atlantic Ocean. It was close enough to New York City so that on weekends the husbands could drive out to be with their families. But during the week, the mothers were alone with their children.

Gerry worried that if a child got into trouble in the water on the unguarded beach, no one would know what to do. So she got the mothers together with a water safety instructor. Several moms, including Gerry, became certified lifeguards. Then Gerry organized a swimming and sailing program for the children, which goes on until this day. Each summer, Gerry tried to put something in place which would benefit the community.

When she saw that the fire department in Pear Harbor was made up of elderly and retired men, she asked the fire chief to train her and some of the other women as volunteer firefighters. He didn't like the idea, so Gerry went to the elected officials. "If a man in his seventies can put out a fire, why can't able-bodied women learn how to do this?" she asked.

The town officials didn't agree. They did not want to admit women to their fire department. But even though Gerry failed to integrate the Pear Harbor fire department in the early 1970s, by the 1980s, not only "did Pear Harbor have an integrated fire department," said Gerry, "it has had a woman fire chief." The seed for this change in attitude towards what women could do was planted by Geraldine Ferraro before she ever thought of going into politics.

In 1974, Gerry began her legal career as an assistant district attorney in Queens, New York. She was worried at first. It had been fourteen years since she graduated from law school. Could she learn all of the new laws that had been passed since she was a student? Could she prosecute criminals as vigorously as someone with more legal experience? She could, and she did. Gerry was able to catch up in record time because of her ability to learn fast. She created a plan to educate herself and become a top-notch prosecutor. Every day, Gerry made long lists of things she had to do, and she didn't quit until she finished her homework.

In 1975, she was assigned to the new Special Victims Bureau, and in 1977, she was appointed its chief. Her job was to make sure the district attorney's office had a good case against people who committed child abuse, rape, and crimes against senior citizens. Although she had many attorneys working under her, she said, "I felt a responsibility to every victim who came in. If it was a young child or a traumatized senior citizen, I would handle the case myself."

Sometimes Gerry was overwhelmed with emotion when a victim of a particularly brutal crime came to her office. She started thinking about what kinds of new laws there might be to protect citizens. Perhaps she ought to be writing laws instead of prosecuting criminals. Also, in her work, she saw that not only did many poor people commit crimes against helpless citizens, but that the victims themselves were very often poor. The connection between poverty and crime became clear to her.

"I wanted to *solve* problems. I wanted to create opportunities for the poor, for women, for the elderly." One evening she shared her thoughts with her friend Mario Cuomo, who was later elected governor of New York, and his wife, Matilda. Mr. Cuomo was very encouraging.

"Why not run for Congress?" he suggested.

"I'll think about it," Gerry answered.

Just as she had done when she first went back to work, Gerry listed the things she wished to accomplish. If she was elected to Congress, she wanted to create educational opportunities for the poor, get medical attention and a good nutrition program for poor pregnant women, and make her office available to her constituents. She also wanted to make sure criminals got punished. The list went on.

In 1978, Geraldine Ferraro ran for a seat in the U.S. House of Representatives from the Ninth Congressional District in Queens. Three men ran against her in the primary, but she won. The people in her district listened when she told them that she could be tough on criminals. She pointed to her excellent record in the district attorney's office. In November, Gerry had little difficulty beating the Republican.

One of her first acts was to set up a congressional office in her district where people could walk in and find help with their problems. Her office was on the first floor so that the elderly and people with disabilities would not have to climb stairs. Then she set up another small office in a van that traveled through the community three days a week. When Congress was in recess, Gerry came back to her district and held town meetings where people could listen to her and tell her what was on their minds. "We're Here to Help" was her motto.

During her first term in Congress, she served on the Post Office and Civil Service Committee, where she defended the interests of federal workers who lost their jobs due to budget cuts. She also served on the Public Works and Transportation Committee, where she supported bills providing more money for mass transit systems (trains, subways, and buses). This was very important to the people in Gerry's district, most of whom rely on subways and buses in order to get to and from work. She also studied the issues of wage, pension, and retirement account fairness for women. For example, she found that in many public and private places of business, women received lower pension benefits than men. Gerry was a fierce advocate for a woman's right to choose to have an abortion. During her first months in Congress, she called for federal funding of abortions for low-income women. This bill did not pass.

When Gerry ran for reelection in 1980, she won with 73 percent of the vote. During this term, she co-sponsored the Retirement Equity Act, which helped make pension laws free of sex discrimination. The legislation ensured that a homemaker whose husband died before retirement would still be able to receive his pension benefits. The bill also protected the pensions of working women who had taken time out from their jobs to raise families. When President Reagan wanted to cut the funding of a program which provides supplementary meals to poor pregnant women and children under five, Gerry voted to renew the funding. She also voted to give more money to community health centers and programs that would promote good health care for women.

Gerry was not afraid to take stands which differed from those of the Democratic leaders in Congress. For example, she voted in favor of the death penalty for certain kinds of crimes. And she voted for more funding for the Trident nuclear submarine at a time when many Democrats thought too much money was being spent by the military.

In 1982, Geraldine Ferraro was reelected to a third term, again by an overwhelming margin. She was popular with her constituents, who liked her forceful stands on issues as well as the way her staff responded to their problems. She worked to increase funding for Head Start (a preschool program for children from lower-income neighborhoods), bilingual education, and education programs for immigrant children. And Gerry was a co-sponsor of the 1984 Civil Rights Act, which made it illegal for schools that discriminated against minorities to receive federal aid. She voted to establish a federal holiday to honor the great civil rights leader Martin Luther King, Jr. All of these bills passed.

For Gerry, one of the hardest things about being a member of Congress was living away from her family. During the week, she lived in a small apartment in Washington while John and the children stayed in Queens. She usually worked in her office until ten at night. Most of the time, she'd grab a quick hamburger for supper and return to her apartment in time to watch the eleven o'clock news. Then she would go to bed. She hated to come home to the empty apartment. That, she said, goes back to her childhood, when her mother had to work at night and Gerry had to

Gerry campaigns for the Senate in 1992.

stay by herself. "I never showed anyone how lonely I felt. I did what I had to do, and I got through it," she added.

"If it weren't for John, I never would have accomplished what I did," Gerry said. Whenever she thought she was too tired to go on, he would say, "Come on, Gerry, you've got to do it." Gerry said that John "never let me or the kids down."

Her ability to get through tough times would be what she needed most when she was campaigning for the vice-presidency in 1984. Gerry and the Democratic presidential candidate, Walter Mondale, were running against the Republican president and vice-president, Ronald Reagan and George Bush. Naturally, the Republicans wanted to win again.

Gerry knew that her stand on some issues would be controversial, especially those which had to do with women. As a Catholic she opposes abortion, but she feels each woman should be free to follow her own conscience. "Abortion should be a woman's personal decision between her and her church, if she has one, and her God, if she believes in one," she said. She was also in favor of the Equal Rights Amendment. These views brought her a lot of criticism. It was hoped, however, that her tough stand against crime and for keeping America strong militarily would appeal to both men and women voters. But soon after the Democratic convention, there was trouble.

Before Gerry was chosen to run with Walter Mondale, she had to fill out a very long questionnaire. It asked many things about her personal life and also asked if Gerry would let her and John's income tax returns become public. There is no law that says a vice-presidential candidate or his or her spouse has to give out this information. However, Gerry said yes. She didn't know that John didn't want to do this, but there was no way for her to go back on her word.

There were errors in John and Gerry's joint income tax returns, and they had to defend themselves. The reporters kept up the pressure on John. Gerry argued that her family was being unfairly targeted both because she was a woman and because she and John were of Italian descent. She said that the backgrounds of the *wives* of presidential and vice-presidential candidates were always treated with respect. John and Gerry paid the taxes that had been questioned, but still the attacks didn't stop.

Even if Geraldine Ferraro had not been having trouble over these problems, it is doubtful that the Democrats would have won the presidential election in 1984. President Reagan and Vice-President Bush were popular. The majority of Americans admired both men and wanted to vote for them again.

But Gerry did not for one moment stop campaigning or give up hope. Between the beginning of October and Election Day on November 6, 1984, she traveled over thirty thousand miles. Once she campaigned in eight states in two days. Now winning wasn't the issue. History was. And everywhere she went, the crowds were huge. She told them, "My candidacy is not just for me. It's for everyone. My candidacy says America believes in equality."

To her and the Democratic party's disappointment, Ronald Reagan and George Bush were overwhelmingly reelected to their second terms as president and vice-president of the United States.

Since the election, Gerry has been in great demand all over the country as a speaker. She has also taught at the Institute of Politics at Harvard University's John F. Kennedy School of Government and served as president of the International Institute for Women's Political Leadership. In 1992, she ran in the New York State primary as a candidate for the United States Senate, but she lost by less than one-half of one percent of the vote.

But Geraldine Ferraro's place in American history is secure. By becoming the Democratic candidate for vice-president of the United States, she did something no American woman had done before. It will always remain a great achievement, both for her personally and for all women. "Someone had to be first," Geraldine Ferraro said. "And I was the one."

The Ferraro family at the Democratic National Convention in 1984.
From left: John, Jr., Gerry, John, Donna, Laura.

Bryna J. Fireside at work in 1993.

HOW I WROTE THIS BOOK

Even before I chose the ten congresswomen whose stories appear in this book, I knew I'd include Jeannette Rankin, the first woman elected to Congress. She had been a heroine of mine ever since I was a child.

Choosing only nine more women was a difficult task.

However, making choices is an important part of the biographer's job. I decided upon certain criteria. Because I wanted to interview each congresswoman (except Jeannette Rankin, who died in 1973), my subjects had to be still living. Each woman had to have achieved something outstanding (if possible, something no other woman had done). And I wanted my subjects to be representative. Since more Democratic than Republican women have been elected to Congress, I chose four Republicans and six Democrats. Although there are more women elected to Congress from the Northeast than from other parts of the country, I wanted congresswomen from many regions. And I wanted to write about women with different religious, ethnic, and racial backgrounds. Finally, I wanted women with a wide range of ideas and opinions on what is best for America.

I wasn't sure how to obtain an interview with one famous woman, let alone nine. But I figured one way was simply to ask. Sometimes I dialed Information for a subject's phone number, called her, and asked if I could interview her either by phone or in person. Other times I wrote letters explaining my work and requesting interviews. Before I did each interview, I learned as much as possible about my subject so that I would not ask questions to which I could easily find the answer in a book or article. I interviewed three women by phone from my office in Ithaca, New York. I traveled to Skowhegan, Maine; New York City; Washington, D.C.; and Bernardsville, New Jersey, to meet with six other subjects. Whether speaking by phone or face-to-face, I used my tape recorder so that I wouldn't miss a word.

Not everyone was willing to speak with me at first. My congressman, Matthew McHugh, helped me contact two of his colleagues in the House and Senate. I learned never to give up—even when someone turned me down more than once. (Four congresswomen did that!) But persistence and determination paid off. I accomplished my goal and interviewed nine famous congresswomen. Their own words appear in this book.

But interviews did not give me all the information I needed. I also explored libraries from Maine to Texas which held the papers of these women as well as other research material. I read letters, books, magazine articles, and newspaper accounts, and interviews that other researchers had had with the congresswomen.

Nearly two years elapsed before I gathered all the interviews and completed enough research to write these ten biographies. It took another year before I was satisfied with what I'd written. But from start to finish, this was a marvelous adventure. To meet and write about each of these resolute and courageous women was one of the greatest pleasures I have known.

SELECTED BIBLIOGRAPHY

In addition to my interviews with the congresswomen and many articles I read in the *New York Times, Washington Post, Time, Newsweek,* the *Denver* (Colorado) *Post,* the *Nation,* the *Daily Texan,* and more than thirty other publications from around the nation, the following sources proved particularly useful:

Abzug, Bella. *Bella! Ms. Abzug Goes to Washington.* New York: Saturday Review Press, 1972.

Amer, Mildred L. *Women in the United States Congress.* Congressional Research Service Report for Congress. Washington, D.C.: The Library of Congress, April 10, 1991.

Brownmiller, Susan. *Shirley Chisholm: A Biography.* Garden City, N.Y.: Doubleday, 1970.

Bryant, Ira B. *Barbara Charline Jordan: From the Ghetto to the Capitol.* Houston, Texas: D. Armstrong, 1977.

Chisholm, Shirley. *The Good Fight.* New York: Harper & Row, 1973.

_____. *Unbought and Unbossed.* Boston: Houghton Mifflin, 1970.

Davis, Flora. *Moving the Mountain: The Women's Movement in America Since 1960.* New York: Simon & Schuster, 1991.

Faber, Doris. *Bella Abzug.* New York: Lothrop, Lee & Shepard, 1976.

Fenwick, Millicent. *Speaking Up.* New York: Harper & Row, 1982.

Ferraro, Geraldine, with Linda Bird Francke. *Ferraro: My Story.* New York: Bantam Books, 1985.

Fireside, Bryna. Interview with Dr. Thomas Freeman, Barbara Jordan's debate coach at TSU. Houston, Texas. March 15, 1991.

_____. Interview with Cecilia Hatfield, Historian, Bureau of Engraving and Printing. Washington, D.C. March 17, 1992.

_____. Interview with Professor Otis King, Barbara Jordan's debating partner at TSU. Houston, Texas. March 15, 1991.

Gertzog, Irwin N. *Congressional Women: Their Recruitment, Treatment and Behavior.* New York: Praeger, 1984.

Giles, Kevin S. *Flight of the Dove: The Story of Jeannette Rankin.* Beaverton, Ore.: Touchstone Press, 1980.

Harris, Ted Carlton. *Jeannette Rankin: Suffragist, First Woman Elected to Congress, and Pacifist.* New York: Arno Press, 1982.

Haskins, James. *Barbara Jordan.* New York: Dial Press, 1977.

_____. *Fighting Shirley Chisholm.* New York: Dial Press, 1975.

Hayes, Roland C. Interview with Barbara Jordan, March 28, 1974. Oral History Project at the National Archives, Lyndon Baines Johnson Library, University of Texas, Austin, Texas.

Jordan, Barbara, and Shelby Hearon. *Barbara Jordan: A Self-Portrait.* Garden City, N.Y.: Doubleday, 1979.

Josephson, Hannah. *Jeannette Rankin: First Lady in Congress.* Indianapolis: Bobbs-Merrill, 1974.

Lee, Essie E. *Women in Congress.* New York: Julian Messner, 1979.

Rankin, Jeannette. Letters (1917) from Jeannette Rankin, Carrie Chapman Catt, and Samuel Gompers to Joseph Ralph, director of the Bureau of Engraving and Printing; Secretary of the Treasury William McAdoo; and President Woodrow Wilson about women's working conditions at the bureau during World War I. National Archives, Washington, D.C.

Rankin, Jeannette. "What We Women Should Do." *Home Journal,* August 17, 1917.

_____. "Why I Voted Against the War." Undated. Jeannette Rankin Papers. Schlesinger Library, Radcliffe College, Cambridge, Mass.

Scheader, Catherine. *Shirley Chisholm: Teacher and Congresswoman.* Hillside, N.J.: Enslow, 1990.

Schroeder, Pat. *Champion of the Great American Family.* New York: Random House, 1989.

Sicherman, Barbara, Carol Green Hurd, et al., eds. *Notable American Women: The Modern Period. A Biographical Dictionary.* Cambridge, Mass.: Harvard University Press, 1980.

Smith, Margaret Chase. *A Declaration of Conscience.* New York: Doubleday, 1972.

_____. "Washington and You," daily syndicated column in *Lewiston* (Maine) *Sun,* August 1950–September 1951.

Uglow, Jennifer S., ed. *The Continuum Dictionary of Women's Biography.* New York: Continuum, 1989.

U.S. Congress, Joint Committee on Printing. *Biographical Directory of the U.S. Congress, 1774–1989.* Washington, D.C.: U.S. Government Printing Office, 1989.

U.S. House of Representatives, Office of the Historian. *Women in Congress, 1917–1990.* (Prepared under the direction of the Commission on the Bicentenary of the U.S. House of Representatives.) Washington, D.C.: U.S. Government Printing Office, 1991.

Warford, Pamela Neal. *"Margaret Chase Smith: In Her Own Words"* (oral history transcript, copyright 1990). Margaret Chase Smith Oral History. Schlesinger Library, Radcliffe College, Cambridge, Mass. The two quotations from Ms. Smith on p. 40 are from pp. 165 and 162 of the Warford interviews.

INDEX